שָׁלוֹם יִשְׂרָאֵל

מִיכָל גֶּפְט

Shalom Israel

Learn Hebrew Conversation through a Modern Israel Connection

Michelle Geft

Shalom Israel - Learn Hebrew Conversation through a Modern Israel Connection
Published by Hebrew Basics
© 2018 Michelle Geft
Monte Nido, CA
All rights reserved
Manufactured in the United States of America
ISBN-13: 978-0-9991405-7-4

This book has a free companion site that can be found at:
www.HebrewBasics.com

Note to educators:
Please contact me directly for discounted bulk orders.

Thank you to Orly Lavi Travish of 972education.com for your professional input, suggestions, and edits throughout the process of this workbook. I am grateful to Lior Geft and Mira Rosenthal for always being available with your time and expertise to edit my work. Thank you, Professor Zvi Zohar and Dr. Michal Ben Ya'akov for sharing multiple resources on Sephardi/ Mizrahi Jewry. Appreciation for Dr. Ivor Geft, Judy Kaufman and my mom for helping with translations. Thank you, Phil Buckman, Anat and Phil Golan, Moshe and Limor Pinz, and Orly Lavi Travish for their time to record and for the use of their voices in the video companions to the conversations. I would also like to thank Yoram Shamir, The National Library of Israel, and Yael at Degania Aleph for your time, information, permissions and support.

Please note: Articles, web sites and videos that you are linked to from this book are not the property of Michelle Geft, Shalom Israel or Hebrew Basics (unless stated in the video itself). The articles, web sites and videos are outside entities and should be credited as such. They are suggested links to explore, research and learn from outside the capacity of this workbook. Videos that are stated as the property of Michelle Geft, Shalom Israel and Hebrew Basics can be used for educational purposes only - I release rights to anyone who uses them in this capacity and credits them accordingly.

A Note From The Author

This workbook is intended for students who can read and write the Hebrew alphabet (the Aleph- Bet) and are familiar with the vowels. My other workbook, "Read, Write, Recite Hebrew," is designed as a prerequisite to this workbook.

Throughout this workbook you will find QR codes (like the one at the bottom of this page), please use your phone to read them. Most phones do not need an application. You simply point your camera at the code, and a link should pop up on your screen. Click the link to explore. If you do not have access to a phone or a QR code reader, please visit www.HebrewBasics.com and go to the Shalom Israel page. Once you are on the correct webpage, scroll down to find the conversation you are on. There is a corresponding link online to every QR code link in the book. The links will open further dialogue through online outlets such as videos, images, articles, and information for enhancing the learner experience. These links are all outside entities and should be credited as such. An animated video, produced by Hebrew Basics, is available for each conversation - click on it to see and hear the conversation.

Thank you for purchasing this workbook, as always, I do hope it exceeds your expectations.

Enjoy your studies,
Michelle

This QR Code will take you to the correct page for the free online companion.
Bookmark this page for further use throughout this book.

Create an icon on your phone for the site so you can access it with the touch of your finger:
For iPhone, when the site is up, "share" the web site and choose "add to home screen."
For Android, when the site is up, tap on the "menu" button and "add to home screen."

CONTENTS

Use this QR code to be connected to the web page that will have all the links to conversations and further research for this book. Bookmark this page for use throughout this book.

www.HebrewBasics.com

The *Aleph Bet* , The Hebrew Alphabet: (Read chart from right to left.)

Value	Sound	Written	Printed	Name
1	A/silent	lc	א	Aleph
2	B	ව	בּ	Bet
2	V	ව	ב	Vet
3	G	ﻉ	ג	Gimmel
4	D	ﻭ	ד	Dalet
5	H	ﻭ	ה	Hay (Heh)
6	V	l	ו	Vav
7	Z	ﻝ	ז	Zayin
8	H̲	ﻥ	ח	H̲et
9	T	ﻭ	ט	Tet
10	Y	'	י	Yud (Yod)
20	K	ﻭ	כּ	Kaf
20	H̲	ﻭ	כ	H̲af
20	H̲/K	ﻭ	ך	H̲af Sofit
30	L	ﻭ	ל	La'med
40	M	א	מ	Mem
40	M	ρ	ם	Mem Sofit
50	N	ﻝ	נ	Noon
50	N	l	ן	Noon Sofit
60	S	ﻭ	ס	Same<u>h</u>
70	A/silent	ﻭ	ע	Ayin
80	P	ﻭ	פּ	Pay (Peh)
80	F	ﻭ	פ	Fay (Feh)
80	F	ﻭ	ף	Fay Sofit
90	Tz	ﻭ	צ	Tzadi
90	Tz	ﻭ	ץ	Tzadi Sofit
100	K	ﻭ	ק	Koof (Kof)
200	R	ﻭ	ר	Resh
300	Sh	ﻭ	שׁ	Shin
300	S	ﻭ	שׂ	Sin
400	T	ﻭ	ת	Tav

REVIEW

The Vowels:

The vowels in the *Aleph Bet* are not letters but marks that appear under, above or in the middle of the letters. Once reading is advanced, vowels are not included in texts; they are used only to teach and to clarify literature or holy scriptures. (Read chart from right to left.)

as in:	Sounds like:	Looks like:		Name:	
<u>A</u>qua	ah	אָ	ָ	*Kamatz*	קָמָץ
<u>A</u>qua	ah	אַ	ַ	*Pata<u>h</u>*	פַּתַ<u>ח</u>
R<u>e</u>d	eh	אֶ	ֶ	*Segol*	סֶגּוֹל
R<u>e</u>d/Gr<u>ey</u>	eh	אֵ	ֵ	*Tzeireh*	צֵירֶה
Gr<u>ee</u>n	ee	אִ	ִ	*Heerik*	חִירִיק
Bl<u>ue</u>	oo	אֻ	ֻ	*Kubootz*	קֻבּוּץ
Bl<u>ue</u>	oo	אוּ	וּ	*Shurook*	שׁוּרֵק
<u>O</u>range	oh	וֹ / אֹ	ֹ	*Holam*	חוֹלָם

(The *Kamatz* you see above is sometimes pronounced "oh," it is called a *Kamatz Katan,* or a small *kamatz.*)

Diphthong:

When the letter *Yud* is without a vowel and follows a letter with a vowel, it adds the "y" sound to the vowel.

Sounds like:	Looks like:	
eye	אַי	יַ
ooy	אוּי	וּי
ay	אֵי	יֵ
oy	אוֹי	וֹי

REVIEW

The *Shva*:

The *Shva* is not a vowel but sometimes acts and looks like one. There are quite a few rules for the *Shva* but, to keep it simple for the purpose of this workbook, here is the *Shva* in a nutshell:

Shva Nah, שְׁוָא נָח - Resting *Shva*: If it's in the middle or the end of the word, you do not pronounce it, it is simply clarifying the end of a syllable. The letters Hay (ה), Het (ח), and Ayin (ע) rarely use a Shva Nah. The Aleph (א) never uses it.

Shva Na, שְׁוָא נָע - Verbal *Shva*: If the *Shva* is at the beginning of the word, it sounds like "i" as in Indigo and/or if there are two *Shva*s in a row anywhere in the word, the first will be a *Shva Nah* and is silent and the second one is a Shva Na and is pronounced, because the first one is clarifying the end of the syllable and the second one begins the next syllable. The letters Aleph (א) Hay (ה), Het (ח), and Ayin (ע) never use a Shva Na.

(Read chart from right to left)

as in:	Sounds like:	Looks like:		Name:	
Indigo	i	בְּ	ְ	Shva	שְׁוָא

The *Hataf* vowels :

Because the letters *Aleph* (א), *Hay* (ה), *Het* (ח), and *Ayin* (ע) do not use the *Shva*, we use *Hataf vowels* to compensate. You will only find the *Hataf* vowels under these four letters.

(Read chart from right to left)

as in:	Sounds like:	Looks like:		Name:	
Orange	oh	אֳ	ֳ	Hataf Kamatz	חֲטַף קָמָץ
Aqua	ah	אֲ	ֲ	Hataf Patah	חֲטַף פַּתָח
Red	eh	אֱ	ֱ	Hataf Segol	חֲטַף סֶגוֹל

Notice that the *Hataf Patah* and *Hataf Segol* sound the same as the stand alone *Patah* and *Segol* vowels. The *Hataf Kamatz* is not the regular *Kamatz* but is the *Kamatz Katan* which is found infrequently in the Hebrew language, and is pronounced "oh".

REVIEW

End Letters:

In Hebrew, the word "*sof*" means "end." A "*sofit*" letter is when a letter takes on a different form at the end of a word.   There are only five letters that have an end letter (*sofit*) they are the *Kaf, Mem, Nun, Pay,* and *Tzadi.*

Kaf / Haf/ Haf Sofit	ך / כ / כּ
Mem / Mem Sofit	ם / מ
Noon / Noon Sofit	ן / נ
Pay / Fay / Fay Sofit	ף / פ / פּ
Tzadi / Tzadi Sofit	ץ / צ

Letter Families:

There are seven "letter families" in the *Aleph Bet.*
Each version of the letter in the "letter family" has the same numerical value.
A few differ in sound based on the *dagesh* (dot in the letter).
Five of the letters have an "end letter" or as we learned above, a *sofit*.

Bet / Vet	ב / בּ
Kaf / Haf/ Haf Sofit	ך / כ / כּ
Mem / Mem Sofit	ם / מ
Noon / Noon Sofit	ן / נ
Pay / Fay / Fay Sofit	ף / פ / פּ
Tzadi / Tzadi Sofit	ץ / צ
Shin / Sin	שׂ / שׁ

REVIEW

The *Dagesh*:

The *dagesh* is the dot in the middle of the letter. *Dagesh* (דָּגֵשׁ) in Hebrew means "stress" or "emphasis." A *dagesh* will bring emphasis to a part of the word.

When you have a *dagesh* in the letters Bet - בּ, Gimmel - גּ, Dalet - דּ, Kaf - כּ, Pay - פּ, Tet - תּ, originally it would change the pronunciation of the letters. In modern Hebrew dialect however, only the *Kaf, Bet* and *Pay* have pronunciation changes. This is called the *Dagesh Kal*.

פ / פּ	כ / כּ	ב / בּ
Fay / Pay	Haf / Kaf	Vet / Bet

When any of the letters Bet (בּ), Gimmel (גּ), Dalet (דּ), Kaf (כּ), Pay (פּ), or Tav (תּ) are at the beginning of a word or the beginning of a syllable, after *Shva Nah* (שְׁוָא נָח), a Dagesh Kal is placed in them. Only these six letters receive a *Dagesh Kal*.

The other *dagesh* is called *Dagesh Hazak*, it can be found in every letter except the gutturals; *Aleph* (א), *Hay* (ה), *Het* (ח), *Ayin* (ע) and the letter *Resh* (ר). There are many rules for the *dagesh*, but we will not discuss them because the rules are attached to grammar which we do not cover in this workbook.

Note: You may see the letter *Hay* with a dot, הּ, at the end of a word, this is not a *dagesh*, but a *mappiq*, it simply gives the *Hay* (ה) a consonantal force and lets you know that the word is a combination of two words.
There are a handful of roots in the Hebrew language that have a *mappiq* too. ex. ג.ב.ה.

Please visit www.HebrewBasics.com for audio/video companions

Video companions
for review section

אֵלִי: שָׁלוֹם¹, אֲנִי² אֵלִי. אֲנִי יֶלֶד.³

רָחֵל: שָׁלוֹם, אֲנִי רָחֵל. אֲנִי יַלְדָה⁴. וּמִי⁵ᐟ⁶ אַתְּ⁷?

לֵאָה: אֲנִי לֵאָה. מִי אַתָּה⁸?

דָנִיאֵל: אֲנִי דָנִיאֵל.

אֵלִי, רָחֵל, לֵאָה, דָנִיאֵל: וְזֹאת⁹ הַשָׂפָה¹⁰ᐟ¹¹ הָעִבְרִית¹²

Watch this conversation

Students learning Hebrew in Ulpan,1955
Photo Credit: Moshe Pridan,1955. Wikipedia Commons

מִלוֹן

1. שָׁלוֹם -hello, goodbye, peace
2. אֲנִי - (am) I
3. יֶלֶד - boy
4. יַלְדָה - girl
5. וְ... / וּ... * - and
6. מִי - who (is/are)
7. אַתְּ - you (f.s.)
8. אַתָּה - you (m.s.)
9. זֹאת - this / that (f.s)
10. הָ... / הַ... * - the
11. שָׂפָה - language
12. עִבְרִית - Hebrew

*The words "and" & "the" are represented in Hebrew by adding one letter in front of a word. These words in Hebrew are not stand alone words. You will see more examples of this in upcoming conversations.

Graffiti by Urban-Deco ועדת-קישוט

When Eliezer Ben Yehuda was a young boy, his father read to him in Hebrew and he developed a love for the language. At the time, Hebrew was only used in prayers, literature and for studying the Jewish scriptures. As Eliezer became educated, he decided that Hebrew should be the spoken language of the Jewish people. Many people opposed his idea but he believed in it. He worked many years to create a new Hebrew dictionary. To create the dictionary, he used words from the *Tanah* (scriptures), and other Hebrew literature. He also created new words for objects and ideas that were modern. He spoke only in Hebrew to his family and also wrote a Hebrew newspaper. Eliezer Ben Yehuda was a key figure in the revival of Hebrew into a modern language.

Now, Hebrew is one of the national languages of Israel. Throughout history, Jews would adapt Hebrew from the *Torah* to the languages spoken in the environment in which they lived. For example Yiddish is a combination of Hebrew and German and Ladino is a combination of Hebrew and Spanish. Jews now have a common language among the entire nation, worldwide, in gratitude mostly to Eliezer Ben Yehuda.

Info and video about Ben Yehuda

Hebrew song about Ben Yehuda

Photo Credit: Shlomo Narinsky, first published 1918 in Jerusalem.

Match the phrases:

I (am) a girl	שָׁלוֹם
hello/ goodbye/	אַתְּ יַלְדָּה
peace you (are) a boy	אֲנִי יֶלֶד
who are you (m.s.)	אֲנִי יַלְדָּה
you (are) a girl	אַתָּה יֶלֶד
I (am) a boy	מִי אַתָּה

Write these words in handwriting:

(You don't have to write the vowels. See below for help.)

1. שָׁלוֹם _____

2. אֲנִי יַלְדָּה _____

3. אֲנִי יֶלֶד _____

4. זֹאת עִבְרִית _____

5. מִי אַתְּ? _____

א ב ג ד ה ו ז ח ט י כ ך ל מ ם נ ן ס ע פ ף ץ צ ק ר ש ת

Conversation One
The Language

Match the picture to the word:

1. עִבְרִית

2. יַלְדָה

3. יֶלֶד

א ב ג

4. שָׁלוֹם

Write these phrases in Hebrew:

1. Hello, I (am a) boy. _____

2. Who (are) you (f.s.)? _____

3. This (is) the Hebrew language. _____

4. You (are a) girl. _____

5. Peace. _____

Hebrew Quiz:

In the Yishuv (the Jewish, settled land before 1948), there was a debate about what the official language of the schools and the universities should be. Many argued it should be Hebrew because they were trying to build a national language for the Jewish people. However, the academic committee of the time thought the language of general studies should be German because German was the language of the academia and sciences of the time. Eliezer Ben Yehuda took a big part in the debate arguing that Hebrew should, of course, be the language that all education in Israel should be taught in. This event is referred to as "The Language War (of 1913)," מִלְחֶמֶת הַשָּׂפוֹת.

> ## גלוי דעת
>
> הקורטוריום של הטכניקום בברלין החליט, שכל המדעים הכלליים בבית־הספר הריאלי ובטכניקום בחיפה לא ילמדו בעברית כי אם בלשון זרה. ההחלטה זו היא התנקשות בנפש האומה העברית ואנו חושבים אותה לאסון לאומי.
>
> אין אנחנו מתנגדים ללמוד לשון זרה איזו שהיא על בוריה בבתה"ס העברים פא", אבל אין הלשון הזרה רשאית לתפום מקום שפת ההוראה, כשם שאין לה זכות זו בבתה"ס של כל עם ועם.
>
> דור שלם עבד בעד תחית שפתנו בתור שפת ביה"ס ושפת החיים, ואנחנו לא נתן להעבירנו על לשוננו, כשם שלא נתן שיעבירונו על דתנו.
>
> הלשון הוא נשמת העם: תחת שפתנו: הוא יסוד הכרתו בתחת עמנו.
>
> כדי שאחדים יכירו בזכות לשוננו, נתן שעם ישראל יגן על שפת ישראל ויביא אותה לידי שלטון גמור בכל בתה"ס בארץ ישראל.
>
> הלשון העברית שהיא הקשר הטבעי בין כל בני עמנו מחויבת להיות שפת הלמודים בכל בתה"ס שלנו, בין של החרדים ובין של אינם חרדים.
>
> השפה העברית קדושה לנו ואנו נלחם בעדה כאשר נלחמו אבותינו בכל זמן בעד קדשי האומה.
>
> טירם המורים—דר. י. לוריא
>
> ועד הלשון —א. בן־יהודה
>
> הועד לחזוק החנוך העברי בארץ־ישראל:
>
> סניף ירושלים—דר. יצחק לוי, דר. יעקב סגל
>
> סניף יפו   —מ. דיזנהוף, דר. ח. בוגרשוב
>
> סניף חיפה —ש. פבזנר, דר. א. אירבן

This poster was created and disseminated to promote the use of Hebrew in the Yishuv.

***

You can find the translation of this poster on the next page.

***

Can you find Ben Yehuda's name?

Learn more about The Language War.

What language do you think the schools in Israel should have been teaching in?
Do you think the same for today? Why?

_____

Note: Some of the Ultra Orthodox of the time were opposed to using Hebrew as a modern language because they believed (and some still believe) that Hebrew is a holy language to be used only for *Torah*, *t'filla*, and Jewish Scriptures.

_____

Here is the translation of the Hebrew poster on the page to your right:

OPINION PIECE

The board of governors of the Technikum in Berlin decided that all of the general science subjects in the Reali School in the Technikum in Haifa should not be taught in Hebrew but rather in a foreign language. This decision is an attack on the soul of the Hebrew nation and we see it as a national disaster.

We have no objection to the teaching of any foreign language in the Hebrew schools in the land of Israel, but the foreign language may not take the place of the language of instruction, as would be the case in other nations.

An entire generation worked for the revival of our language as the language of instruction and of everyday life. And we will not agree to giving up our language, just as we would not agree to give up on our religion.

Language is the soul of a nation: The revival of our language is the source of our nation's existence and a necessary foundation for the revival of our nation.

In order for others to recognize the legitimacy of our language, it is essential for the people of Israel to defend the language of Israel and have it be the authoritative language of the schools in all of the land of Israel.

The language of Israel is the natural connection between all the people of our nation. It is imperative to be the language of studies in all of our schools, in the orthodox and in the non-orthodox schools.

The Hebrew language is holy to us and we will fight for it as our forefathers fought throughout history for all things holy of our nation.

Chairman of teachers: Dr. Luria
Committee of Languages: E. Ben-Yehuda
Committee of Hebrew education in the land of Israel:
Branch of Yerushalayim: Dr. Yitzhak Levi, Dr. Yaacov Sigal.
Branch of Jaffa: Mr.Dizenhoff, Dr. H. Bugreshoff
Branch of Haifa: Sh.Pozner, Dr. A. Ayerbach

Photo on opposite page and this translation is from The National Library of Israel web site.

Art Project:

Try to find an Israeli newspaper or magazine. Look through it to find the words we learned in this conversation. Cut the words out and paste them below.
If you can't find the words, cut out letters to make the words.
Use your imagination to make a collage or a picture.

Use your imagination:

Eliezer Ben Yehuda had to make up words in Hebrew for modern culture.
Using Hebrew and English as your base:

Can you make up a word in Hebrew? _____

What does your word mean?_____

What is your rationale? _____

Include your new word in your art piece above.

Who do you think this street is named after?

All the street signs in Israel are written in Hebrew, Arabic and English.

Discussion:

Why do you think the street signs are written in
these three languages?

שִׂיחָה שְׁתַּיִם

הֶחָזוֹן

זְאֵב: רוֹנִית, אַתְּ מְדַבֶּרֶת[1] עִבְרִית?

רוֹנִית: כֵּן,[2] אֲנִי מְדַבֶּרֶת קְצַת[3] עברית. אֲנִי גַם[4] מְדַבֶּרֶת אַנְגְלִית[5].

אַתָּה מְדַבֵּר[6] עברית?

זְאֵב: כֵּן, אני מְדַבֵּר עברית. אֵיפֹה[7] אַת גָּרָה[8]?

Watch this conversation

רוֹנִית: אני גָּרָה בְּיִשְׂרָאֵל.[10/9] אתה גַם גָּר[11] בְּיִשְׂרָאֵלִי?

זְאֵב: לֹא[12], אני לֹא גָּר בְּיִשְׂרָאֵל, אני גָּר בְּאֵירוֹפָּה.[13]

מִלּוֹן

8. גָּרָה - live (f.s.)		1. מְדַבֶּרֶת - speak (f.s.)
9. בְּ... * - in		2. כֵּן - yes
10. יִשְׂרָאֵל - Israel		3. קְצַת - little
11. גָּר - live (m.s.)		4. גַם - also
12. לֹא - no, not, do not		5. אַנְגְלִית - English
13. אֵירוֹפָּה - Europe		6. מְדַבֵּר - speak (m.s.)
		7. אֵיפֹה - where

*The word "in" is represented in Hebrew by adding one letter in front of a word. This word in Hebrew is not a stand alone word. You will see more examples of this in upcoming conversations.

Theodore "Benyamin Ze'ev" Herzl was a pioneer of Modern Israel. He lived in Vienna. Herzl was a journalist who was connected with politicians and other influential people. He started to see through his reporting that the social climate for the Jews in Europe was not good and getting worse. There was also a big push for nationalism throughout the country. Herzl took a leadership role in a movement called Zionism and held the first Zionist conference in 1897 in Basel, Switzerland. The Zionist movement sought to find approval for Jews to have a land of their own. They wanted to return to the land of Israel, the land of their forefathers and the land they pray towards every day. Jews began moving to Israel in more significant numbers. Many wealthy Jews in Europe supported the building of a Jewish nation. These pioneering Jews cleaned swamps, built farms, worked the land and began to create a foundation to rebuild a Jewish society in the land of Israel.

In 1948, about fifty years after Theodore Herzl's vision and leadership, Israel became a state. A Jewish state was born through efforts of the Zionist movement, the United Nations, and groups of Jews who fought for the land, both physically and intellectually.

Watch a video on Theodore Herzl

Herzl is known for his saying :

"If you will it, it is not a dream"

"אִם תִּרְצוּ, אֵין זוֹ אַגָּדָה"

Listen to a popular camp song using

Practice the vocabulary, match the phrases:

and, also	1. גָּר בְּ...
lives in (f.s.)	2. גָּרָה בְּ..
speak (f.s.)	3. גַּם
speak (m.s.)	4. מְדַבֶּרֶת
lives in (m.s.)	5. קְצָת
a little	6. מְדַבֵּר

Circle the correct pronoun then translate:
Refer to the vocabulary you learned so far.

1. אַתָּה   אַתְּ   מְדַבֶּרֶת _____

2. אַתָּה   אַתְּ   יֶלֶד _____

3. אַתָּה   אַתְּ   גָּרָה _____

4. אַתָּה   אַתְּ   מְדַבֵּר _____

5. אַתָּה   אַתְּ   גָּר _____

6. אַתָּה   אַתְּ   יַלְדָּה _____

Conversation Two

The Vision

1. כֵּן **לֹא** - יַלְדָּה

2. כֵּן **לֹא** - יִשְׂרָאֵל

3. כֵּן **לֹא** - שָׁלוֹם

4. כֵּן **לֹא** - עִבְרִית

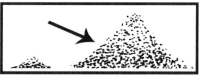

5. כֵּן **לֹא** - שָׂפָה

6. כֵּן **לֹא** - קְצָת

Write a short conversation using the words you learned so far:

אִילָן: _____

נֹעָה: _____

אִילָן: _____

Hebrew Quiz:

שִׂיחָה שְׁתַּיִם
הֶחָזוֹן

Research and discuss:

At the beginning of the twentieth century, Zionism was on the rise. On the following page, you will find five documents that give various perspectives on Zionism during the turn of the century.

Zionism was a topic discussed around the world. In a letter from Morocco, a gentleman asks The World Zionist Organization about the status of the Zionist movement because, as he explains in his letter, the situation in Morocco was not suitable for the Jews (1903). Theodore Herzl's letter to his friend expresses how difficult the Zionist initiative is and how he is making enemies and friends along the way (1896). Herzl worked very hard to make connections in Europe to get support for the Zionist movement and to lobby for Israel (then Palestine) to be the homeland for the Jews. This persistence and continuous work led to The Balfour Declaration (1917). In the Balfour Declaration, Sir Balfour writes a letter to Lord Rothschild expressing the Majesty's government support for a homeland for the Jewish people in Palestine.

Meanwhile, in America, William E. Blackstone, a Methodist and an evangelist, wrote the Blackstone Memorial (1891) that was presented to President Harrison. The Blackstone Memorial, which was entitled "Palestine for the Jews," was signed by 413 prominent Americans and business leaders including J.P. Morgan and John Rockefeller. It was a significant factor in America's support for The Balfour Declaration of 1917. Louis Dembitz Brandeis and Nathan Straus called William E. Blackstone the Father of Zionism because his work came before the work of Herzl's. Lastly, you will find an article written by Rashid Mouhamad Rida, an Arab journalist, who warns the Arabs about the Jews and their organizations. He states that the Arabs ought not to take the Jews lightly because they will overtake Palestine as their homeland. There are many supporters and opponents of Zionism until today.

Discuss with your class how these primary sources give you a first person peak back into time. What can you learn from reading them? Can you further your research from here?

للهود جمعيات ملية كثيرة – ولا نجاح للأمم الا بالجعيات – ولم
نسمع بذكر الجعية الصهيونية الا من نحو خمس سنين وهي جمعية سياسية
غرضها الاستيلاء على البلاد المقدسة لتكون مقر ملكهم وعرش سلطانهم
وقد جاء ذكر هذه الجمعية فى العدد السادس من منار السنة الاولى
(ص ٤٤ و ٤٥) وفيه ان حركة هذه الجمعية ظهرت فجأة فى النمسا والمانيا
ر طلب الملك وانما كانت
خرجين (المنفيّين) الى بلاد
طان آمنين ، وكأنها وثقت
، وقد بعثت منذ اشهر المستمر
مة فى شراء القدس الشريف
نعطافاً . وبعد رجوعه خطب

Palestine for the Jews

COPY OF
MEMORIAL
PRESENTED TO
President Harrison
March 5th, 1891

What shall be done for the Russian Jews? It is both unwise and
Russia concerning her internal
foreigners in her dominions for
that they are a burden upon her
elfare of her peasant population,
n. She is determined that they
lim of Spain, these Ashkenazim
,000,000 of such poor people go?
om for more peasant population.
s will be a tremendous expense,

hem again? According to God's
home—an inalienable possession
force. Under their cultivation it

Foreign Office,
November 2nd, 1917.

Dear Lord Rothschild,

I have much pleasure in conveying to you, on
behalf of His Majesty's Government, the following
declaration of sympathy with Jewish Zionist aspirations
which has been submitted to, and approved by, the Cabinet

"His Majesty's Government view with favour the
establishment in Palestine of a national home for the
Jewish people, and will use their best endeavours to
facilitate the achievement of this object, it being
clearly understood that nothing shall be done which
may prejudice the civil and religious rights of
existing non-Jewish communities in Palestine, or the
rights and political status enjoyed by Jews in any
other country"

I should be grateful if you would bring this
declaration to the knowledge of the Zionist Federation.

Yours

Hochgeehr

Ihr freund
Brief hat
erfreut. Es
augenblicke
des Verdrus
fida Angriy
Sie rühig:
grossen Fel
ich Raum.
habe ich
Freunde!
Zu diesen zähle ich Sie und
schicke Ihnen meine Freangrüsse
Ihr ergebener,
Th Herzl

See these documents enlarged and translated

A TRUE VISIONARY! READ ALL ABOUT IT...

This is taken out of Herzl's diary which was written, in German, on September 3, 1897:

The visionary that he was, he wrote: "If I had to sum up the Basel Congress in one phrase --which I would not do openly-- it would be this: At Basel I founded the Jewish state. If I were to say this today, I would be greeted by universal laughter. In five years, perhaps, and certainly in 50, everyone will see it."

Just over fifty years later, in 1948:

See The Palestine Post front page enlarged

Image used with permission from The Jerusalem Post Archives Department.

Here is a signed photograph of David Ben Gurion, the
first Prime Minister of Israel, while he is declaring the new Jewish state.
A picture of Theodore Benjamin Ze'ev Herzl hangs above him.
It was Herzl's leadership of the Zionist movement that led to the
state the Jews have today.

Watch the
speech

Image courtesy of The Museum of Tolerance in Los Angeles from the Garb Collection.

אֵיתָן: מַאיָה, אֵיפֹה אֵת גרה בישראל ?

מַאיָה: אני גרה בָּעִיר[1\2]. אֵיפֹה אתה גר ?

אֵיתָן: אני גר בְּקִבּוּץ[3] עִם[4] הַמִּשְׁפָּחָה[5] שֶׁלִי[6].
מָה[7] אֵת עוֹשָׂה[8] בָּעִיר ?

מַאיָה: אני סְטוּדֶנְטִית,[9] אני לוֹמֶדֶת[10] בָּאוּנִיבֶרְסִיטָה[11].
מָה אתה עוֹשֶׂה[12] בַּקִבּוּץ ?

אֵיתָן: אני עוֹבֵד[13] בְּבֵית סֵפֶר[14] בַּקִבּוּץ, אני מוֹרֶה[15].

מַאיָה: זֶה[16] יָפֶה[17] מְאוֹד[18]!

אֵיתָן: כֵּן, תּוֹדָה[19].

Watch this conversation

מִלוֹן

11. אוּנִיבֶרְסִיטָה - university	1. בָּ...\ בַּ... - in the
12. עוֹשֶׂה - do / does (m.s.)	2. עִיר - city
13. עוֹבֵד - work/works (m.s.)	3. קִבּוּץ - kibbutz
14. בֵּית סֵפֶר - school	4. עִם - with
15. מוֹרֶה - teacher (m.s.)	5. מִשְׁפָּחָה - family
16. זֶה - this / that (m.s.)	6. שֶׁלִי - my / mine
17. יָפֶה - nice, pretty (m.s.)	7. מָה - what
18. מְאוֹד - very	8. עוֹשָׂה - do / does (f.s.)
19. תּוֹדָה - thank you	9. סְטוּדֶנְטִית - student (f.s.)
	10. לוֹמֶדֶת - learns / learning (f.s.)

Conversation Three
The Kibbutz

In 1918, after World War I, a wave of Jews immigrated to Israel. When a Jew immigrates to Israel, the move is called *aliyah*. Te Jews who made *aliyah* at this time, set up some of the first settlements known as *kibutzim* (community farms). In *kibbutzim*, they raised animals for food, made dairy products and cultivated fruits and vegetables. Some kibbutzim included factories. Everybody worked together, lived together, owned property collectively, and even shared all the profits. The products from the *kibbutzim* fed the community and nearby towns. The kibbutz movement helped build the land, gave jobs and shelter to new immigrants, and brought Jews from different backgrounds together. Jews worked together with their families and established farms, schools, and communities.

The foods produced on a *kibbutz* are sold locally and at the *shuk* (שׁוּק). A *shuk* is like a farmer's market, but they are usually held every day in certain parts of the city. Many of the products from the *kibbutzim* are also sold in local stores. A neighborhood store is called a *ma'kolet* (מַכֹּלֶת), and a supermarket is called a *soo'pare* (סוּפֶּר).

6 min video on the *kibbutz*

A ceremony on an Israeli kibbutz in July 1951. Wikimedia Commons. בני נוער צועדים בעצרת בני הקיבוץ המאוחד

kibbutzim (plural)	קִבּוּצִים	*kibbutz (single)*	קִבּוּץ

שִׂיחָה שָׁלוֹש

הַקִּיבּוּץ

Write the number of the correct word that describes the picture:

1. עִיר

2. מוֹרֶה

3. אֵיפֹה

4. מִשְׁפָּחָה

5. סְטוּדֶנְטִית

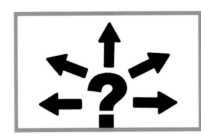

Image courtesy of @emes_shots.

What do these words mean? Circle the "question" words.

לֹא   אַתָּה   אֲנִי   עִם   מִי   אַתְּ   מָה   אֵיפֹה   כֵּן

Write four questions:

Use the "question" words you circled above and the vocabulary you learned so far.

1. _____ ?

2. _____ ?

3. _____ ?

4. _____ ?

Conversation Three
The Kibbutz

Answer these questions in Hebrew:

Use the conversation on page 30.

1. אֵיפֹה מַאיָה גָּרָה ? _____

2. מָה מַאיָה עוֹשָׂה ? _____

3. מִי גָּר בְּקִיבּוּץ ? _____

4. עִם מִי אֵיתַן גָּר ? _____

5. מָה אֵיתַן עוֹשָׂה ? _____

Match the words that have a connection:

כֵּן	זֶה יֶלֶד
אַתָּה	גָּר בְּ...
עִבְרִית	מוֹרֶה בְּ...
קִבּוּץ	אַתְּ
זֹאת יַלְדָּה	לֹא
בֵּית סֵפֶר	שָׂפָה

Translate the matches you found:

_____ / _____   _____ / _____

_____ / _____   _____ / _____

_____ / _____   _____ / _____

Hebrew Quiz:

First Grammar Break

In Hebrew, there are four forms of a noun.
Here are four forms of the noun, "student:"

סְטוּדֶנְטִיוֹת   סְטוּדֶנְטִים   סְטוּדֶנְטִית   סְטוּדֶנְט

female	male	female	male
plural	plural	singular	singular
(f.p.)	(m.p.)	(f.s.)	(m.s.)

In Hebrew, there are four forms of a verb in regular present tense.
Here are four forms of the verb, "learns:"

לוֹמְדוֹת   לוֹמְדִים   לוֹמֶדֶת   לוֹמֵד

female	male	female	male
plural	plural	singular	singular
(f.p.)	(m.p.)	(f.s.)	(m.s.)

If we combine the two pieces of information from above,
you can see how a noun matches a verb.

סְטוּדֶנְט **לוֹמֵד** בָּאוּנִיבֶרְסִיטָה.

סְטוּדֶנְטִית **לוֹמֶדֶת** בָּאוּנִיבֶרְסִיטָה.

סְטוּדֶנְטִים **לוֹמְדִים** בָּאוּנִיבֶרְסִיטָה.

סְטוּדֶנְטִיוֹת _____ בָּאוּנִיבֶרְסִיטָה.

(fill in)

Earlier we learned the Hebrew word for "this" (m.s.) זֶה and (f.s.) זֹאת.
Now that we are learning some plural nouns, let's learn the Hebrew word for
"these / those:": אֵלֶה. אֵלֶה is used for both male and female plural nouns.

Conversation Three
The Kibbutz

The first *kibbutz* to be established in Israel is called *Degania Aleph*. Pioneers moved to the land as early as 1904 and after some trial and error, established the *kibbutz* in 1910. One of the founders, Dr. Arthur Ruppin wrote:

> To the director of the Land of Israel Office, Dr. Arthur Ruppin. Dear Sir, We hereby inform your honor that we have named our new settlement 'Degania', after the five varieties of grains growing here.

The pioneers (*Halutzim*) cleaned and worked the land and grew grains. The unique contribution of *Degania* was that it was a melting pot for many of the Jews from the Diaspora. The residents of Degania gave them food, shelter, work, and a Jewish community. After training on *Degania*, some moved on and set up *kibbutzim* around the country. There are over 250 working *Kibbutzim* in Israel today. Degania was the model for all the *kibbutzim* that followed.

Degania is still a working *kibbutz*. It has a museum, zoo, garden, farm, chicken coop, and a cowshed. They also started a factory that produces industrial tools and distributes them worldwide. Some families who live on the *kibbutz* have small businesses as well.

Visit Degania's web site

Article about *kibbutzim* and high-tech

Research and discuss:

15 min video on the *kibbutz*

There are over 250 *kibbutzim* in Israel today. Find one, using the QR code to the right, and research what it produces. If you are in a classroom, have students research and present different *kibbutzim*.

List of working *kibbutzim* with links

Degania, 1910 - The first *kibbutz*

Degania Aleph, 2002 - A modern *kibbutz*

Pictures above are used with permission from www.Degania.org.il.

This is a poster from the 1950's that promotes the Kibbutz movement.

Today's product of the Hebrew farms

Made in Israel

This table will indicate the loyalty to the country's produce and will clarify every day what the fruit and vegetables of the Hebrew economy are.

We will expand the agricultural settlements and increase aliyah.

Signed with the seal of The Agricultural Department of the Association for Israeli Products.

Every day, always, production of our land.

Image used with permission from Eri Wallish.

Discussion:

1. The *kibbutz* movement was a key player in the *aliyah* movement in the 1900s. Why do you think this was so?

2. Based on the research you did on the previous page and on the discussion you had, how did the *kibbutz* evolve from the early 1900s to now?

שִׂיחָה אַרְבַּע

הַצָּבָא

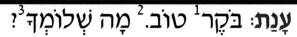

Watch this conversation

עֲנָת: בֹּקֶר[1] טוֹב.[2] מָה שְׁלוֹמְךָ[3]?

תּוֹמֶר: טוֹב מְאוֹד. מָה שְׁלוֹמֵךְ[4]?

עֲנָת: אֲנִי כָּכָה-כָּכָה.[5] מִי זֹאת?

תּוֹמֶר: זֹאת חֲבֵרָה[6] שֶׁלִי. הִיא[7] חַיֶּלֶת[8] בַּצָּבָא.[9]

עֲנָת: סַבָּבָה![10] וּמִי זֶה?

תּוֹמֶר: זֶה נָדָב, הוּא[11] לֹא חַיָּל,[12] אֲבָל[13] הוּא עוֹשֶׂה מִלוּאִים.[14]

עֲנָת: הַיי! מָה הַשֵּׁם[15] שֶׁלָךְ[16]?

גָלִית: הַשֵּׁם שֶׁלִי גָלִית.

עֲנָת: שָׁלוֹם, הַשֵּׁם שֶׁלִי עֲנָת. נָעִים מְאוֹד.[17] מָה אַתֶּם[18] עוֹשִׂים[19] הַיּוֹם[20]?

גָלִית: הַיּוֹם אֲנַחְנוּ[21] הוֹלְכִים[22] לַיָּם,[23/24] וְנָדָב הוֹלֵךְ[25] לַקִבּוּץ.

מִלוֹן

14. מִלוּאִים - (IDF) reserves	1. בֹּקֶר (בוקר) - morning
15. שֵׁם - name	2. טוֹב - good
16. שֶׁלָךְ - your / yours (f.s.)	3. מָה שְׁלוֹמְךָ - how are you (m.s.)
17. נָעִים מְאוֹד - very nice (to meet you)	4. מָה שְׁלוֹמֵךְ - how are you (f.s.)
18. אַתֶּם - you (m.p.)	5. כָּכָה-כָּכָה - so-so
19. עוֹשִׂים - doing / do (m.p.)	6. חֲבֵרָה - friend (f.s.)
20. הַיּוֹם - today	7. הִיא - she (is)
21. אֲנַחְנוּ - we	8. חַיֶּלֶת (חיילת) - soldier (f.s.)
22. הוֹלְכִים - going / go (m.p.)	9. צָבָא - army
23. לַ.../לְ... * - to the	10. סַבָּבָה - awesome
24. יָם - sea	11. הוּא - he (is)
25. הוֹלֵךְ - going / goes (m.s.)	12. חַיָּל (חייל) - soldier (m.s.)
*"to the" is represented by one letter in front of a word.	13. אֲבָל - but

The IDF was established on May 31, 1948, two weeks after the establishment of the State of Israel. The acronym IDF stands for Israel Defense Forces. The Hebrew letters stand for *Tzva ha'haganah le'Yisrael* (צה"ל). It was comprised of several underground organizations that fought for Jewish Independence before 1948, also all acronyms: *Palmach* (פלמ"ח), *Le<u>h</u>i* (לח"י), and *Etzel* (אצ"ל).

When Israeli teenagers turn eighteen, it is mandatory by the state for (most) Israeli citizens to serve in the IDF. There are many ways to serve in the IDF based on your ability and talent. The IDF makes room for all abilities. They have soldiers who serve with autism, down syndrome and many different learning abilities. The IDF empowers everyone to serve in the army using their specialties. There are also opportunities for the physically disabled.

Video of all abilities IDF volunteers

Arab, Druze, and Bedouin citizens also serve in the Israeli Army. They are not obligated to serve, but many volunteer and are welcome by the Jewish Israelis.

Video of non-Jewish IDF volunteer

Mini history of Jewish organizations in Israel who fought for Israel:
- NILI is an acronym for the Hebrew phrase *"Netzah Yisrael Lo Yeshaker,"* meaning "The Eternal One of Israel will not lie." They spied for the British to aid the Jewish cause.
- The Jewish Legion formed a Jewish brigade within the British army.
- The *Haganah* was established on June 12, 1920 to protect the Jewish settlers from Arab mobs. It continued to reinvent itself until 1948 when it became part of the foundation of the IDF. *Palmach (Plugot Ma<u>h</u>atz)*, *Lechi (Lohamei Herut Israel)* and *Etzel (Irgun Tz'va Leumi)* were all Jewish brigades organized to fight for the land of Israel as a homeland for the Jews. They came together (with the *Haganah*) to comprise the IDF.

Video talking about the I.D.F.

In the Israeli Defense Forces, each and every soldier is cared and accounted for. We learned a few pronouns so far. Let's learn all of them so we can account for everyone.

**Fill in the pronouns you learned,
then draw a line from the pronoun to the matching picture**

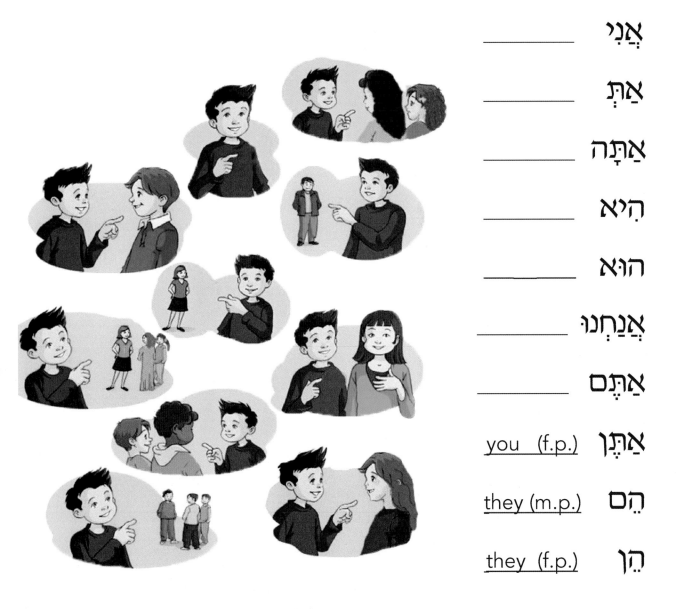

_____	אֲנִי
_____	אַתְּ
_____	אַתָּה
_____	הִיא
_____	הוּא
_____	אֲנַחְנוּ
_____	אַתֶּם
you (f.p.)	אַתֶּן
they (m.p.)	הֵם
they (f.p.)	הֵן

Fill out the crossword puzzle using all the Hebrew pronouns:

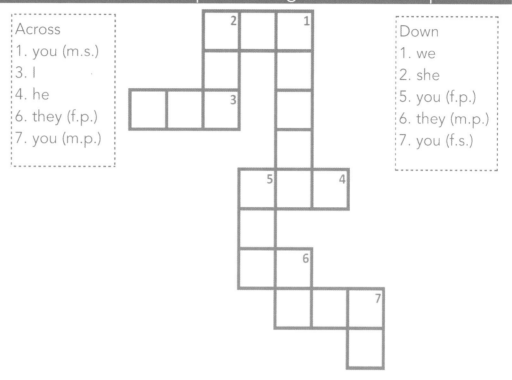

Across
1. you (m.s.)
3. I
4. he
6. they (f.p.)
7. you (m.p.)

Down
1. we
2. she
5. you (f.p.)
6. they (m.p.)
7. you (f.s.)

Circle the correct pronoun:

1. ‏**אני** **אנחנו** עוֹשֶׂה מִלוּאִים.

2. ‏**אני** **אנחנו** הוֹלְכִים לַיַּם.

3. ‏**את** **אתה** יַלְדָה.

4. ‏**אתם** **אתן** לוֹמְדִים בָּאוּנִיבֶרְסִיטָה.

5. ‏**היא** **הוא** חֲבֵרָה שֶׁלִי.

6. ‏**הם** **הן** גָּרוֹת בְּיִשְׂרָאֵל.

Write the correct word or phrase under the pictures:

מִשְׁפָּחָה.　　שָׁלוֹם, הַשֵׁם שֶׁלִי...　　בּוֹקֶר טוֹב.

מִי, מָה, אֵיפֹה.　　שָׁלוֹם.　　אֲנִי חַיָּיל בַּצָּבָא.

אֲנִי עוֹבֵד בַּקִּיבּוּץ.　　זֹאת יַלְדָּה.

_____ .3

GOOD MORNING!
_____ .2

Hello my name is
_____ .1

_____ .4

_____ .5

_____ .8

Image courtesy of Ran Ferdman, CEO Ruhama Field Crops.
_____ .6

_____ .7

Learning to translate:

1. Good morning! _____
2. Very good!_____
3. He is a good friend. _____
4. Very nice! _____
5. This is a soldier (f.s.) _____

Write a conversation using the words you learned so far:

Use the pronouns you learned, include these words in your dialogue:

מָה שְׁלוֹמְךְ - מָה שְׁלוֹמֵךְ - מִי - אֵיפֹה - עוֹשֶׂה - כֵּן - לֹא

אָלוֹן: _____

יוֹנִית: _____

אָלוֹן: _____

יוֹנִית: _____

אָלוֹן: _____

יוֹנִית: _____

Practice reading your conversation and a classmate's conversation.
Create and write a conversation together on another piece of paper.

Hebrew
Quiz:

שִׂיחָה אַרְבַּע

הַצָּבָא

This is *Ru'ah Tza'hal* / The Spirit of *Tza'hal* / *Tza'hal* Code of Ethics

Taken from http://www.jewishvirtuallibrary.org/ruach-tzahal-idf-code-of-ethics

This pamphlet is given to every soldier upon entrance into service. It is read and discussed among new recruits. The IDF is considered one of the most ethical armies in the world. The Code of Ethics was written by, philosopher and linguist, Professor Asa Kasher.

Information & translation of The Code of Ethics:

Conversation Four

The Israeli Defence Forces

In conversation with Asa Kasher, he is asked what stands out in the Code of Ethics of the Israeli Defense Forces. In response, there are two major points that exist in the IDF Code of Ethics that do not appear in other countries' Code of Ethics:

"I read a lot and was indeed fluent in the spirit of the IDF. Some of the values are common to many military forces, but two values suggested were new and to this very day they appear only in our Code of Ethics: (Sanctity of) Human Life, and "Purity of Arms" [restraint of force]. I take both of them to be of Jewish roots."

The original Code of Ethics document included eleven values and thirty-four principles. In 2001, "patriotism" was added as a value and the principles were removed (simply to make it shorter).

Discussion:

Using the QR codes on these two pages, the information written above and any other resources you may find, discuss the following:

What parts of the Code of Ethics stand out to you? What would you add? Do you think these ethics are always being kept by all soldiers? What do you think the repercussions of breaking the Codes of Ethics should be, if any? Are there times when it is necessary to break these codes?

Research more here:

_____

_____

_____

_____

שִׂיחָה חָמֵשׁ

הַמְּדִינָה

עֵדֶן: מֵאֵיפֹה[1] אַת?

לִימוֹר: אֲנִי מֵאַרְצוֹת הַבְּרִית[2]. עַכְשָׁיו[3] אֲנִי גָרָה עַל-יַד[4] בְּאֵר שֶׁבַע. מֵאֵיפֹה אַת?

עֵדֶן: אֲנִי מִירוּשָׁלַיִם, אֲבָל עַכְשָׁיו אֲנִי גָרָה בְּתֵל אָבִיב.   מֵאֵיפֹה אַתָּה?

נֹעַם: אֲנִי מֵחֵיפָה, וַאֲנִי עֲדַיִין[5] גָר בְּחֵיפָה, אֲבָל אִמָּא[6] וְאַבָּא[7] שֶׁלִי (הַהוֹרִים[8] שֶׁלִי) גָרִים[9] בְּטְבֶרְיָה. הָאָח[10] שֶׁלִי גָר בִּצְפַת, וְהָאֲחָיוֹת[11] שֶׁלִי גָרוֹת[12] בְּאֵילַת.

עֵדֶן: הָאָחוֹת[13] שֶׁלִי גַם גָרָה בְּאֵילַת.

לִימוֹר: הַחֲבֵרִים[14] שֶׁלִי גַם גָרִים בְּאֵילַת! יָאלְלָה[15], רוֹצִים[16] לִנְסוֹעַ[17] לְאֵילַת[18]?

עֵדֶן: כֵּן, אֲנִי יְכוֹלָה[19] לִנְסוֹעַ בַּשָׁבוּעַ[20] הַבָּא[21].

נֹעַם: כֵּן, גַם אֲנִי יָכוֹל[22]!

עֵדֶן: אַחְלָה[23]! לְהִתְרָאוֹת[24] בַּשָׁבוּעַ הַבָּא!

נֹעַם, עֵדֶן, לִימוֹר: יָאלְלָה, לְאֵילַת!

Watch this conversation

מִלוֹן

12. גָרוֹת - live (f.p.)		1. מֵ.../מְ.../מִ... - from
13. אָחוֹת - sister		2. אַרְצוֹת הַבְּרִית - United States
14. חֲבֵרִים - friends (m.p.)		3. עַכְשָׁיו - now
15. יָאלְלָה - hurry up / let's go		4. עַל-יָד - next to
16. רוֹצִים - want (m.p.)		5. עֲדַיִין - still
17. לִנְסוֹעַ - to travel		6. אִמָּא - mom/mother
18. לְ... - to		7. אַבָּא - dad / father
19. יְכוֹלָה - able (f.s.)		8. הוֹרִים - parents
20. שָׁבוּעַ - week		9. גָרִים - live (m.p.)
21. הַבָּא - that is coming		10. אָח - brother
22. יָכוֹל - able (m.s.)		11. אֲחָיוֹת - sisters
23. אַחְלָה - awesome		
24. לְהִתְרָאוֹת - see you later		

Find where all the cities mentioned are located :

Mini research and presentation :

Look up a city from the conversation (in groups or individually).
Find out what that city is known for. What interesting facts can you find?
Share your findings with your classmates.

3 min visual of Israel

      Israel is a tiny piece of land that sits on the east coast of the Mediterranean Sea. It takes only six hours to drive from one end of the country to the other. Israel has been around for thousands of years and has been renamed numerous times by the different nations who ruled the area. It was declared a Jewish state in 1948 by the United Nations. The Jews have not had control of the land since 70 C.E. Israel's national anthem, *Hatikva (The Hope)*, expresses this two-thousand-year hope for a return and the joy of being able to call Israel our Jewish homeland once again.

      Jews move to Israel every year to be a part of the modern, Jewish society. When a Jew moves to Israel it is called *Aliyah* (going up). There is a strong Jewish attachment to the land of Israel, from the present moment through time immemorial. Jewish people of all types and level of religious observance live in Israel. The predominant faiths in Israel are Judaism, Islam and Christianity. In Israel, there is freedom of religion to all faiths.

Search and find the words, then translate them:

1. לא _____
2. יפה _____
3. אני _____
4. אתה _____
5. את _____
6. היא _____
7. יאללה _____
8. עכשיו _____
9. שם _____
10. רוצה _____
11. עושה _____
12. יכול _____
13. חברה _____
14. אחלה _____
15. איפה _____
16. מי _____
17. מה _____
18. להתראות _____

Highlight where you would find these cities on the lettered map. Write the name of the city next to your highlight :

חיפה   תל אביב   אילת   ירושלים
צפת   טבריה   באר שבע

שִׂיחָה חָמֵשׁ
הַמְּדִינָה

Answer these questions in Hebrew:

Use the conversation on page 46 .

1. מֵאֵיפֹה לִימוֹר?
_____

2. אֵיפֹה לִימוֹר גָּרָה עַכְשָׁיו?
_____

3. אֵיפֹה הַהוֹרִים שֶׁל נֹעַם גָּרִים?
_____

4. מִי יָכוֹל לִנְסֹעַ לְאֵילַת בַּשָׁבוּעַ הַבָּא?
_____

Write the number of the correct phrase that describes the picture:

_____

1. הַמּוֹרָה עוֹמֶדֶת* עַל-יַד הַיֶּלֶד.
2. הֶחַיִל עוֹמֵד* עַל-יַד הַחַיֶּילֶת.
3. אֲנִי עוֹמֶדֶת עַל-יַד הַחֲבֵרָה שֶׁלִּי.

_____

עוֹמֶדֶת (f.p.) / עוֹמְדִים (m.p.) / עוֹמֵד (m.s.) / עוֹמֶדֶת (f.s.) Stand(s)*
עוֹמְדוֹת

Conversation Five
The State

1. **הִיא**   **הוא**   חֲבֵרָה   _____
2. **אתה**   **את**   מְדַבֶּרֶת   _____
3. **אתם**   **אתן**   גָּרִים   _____
4. **הם**   **הן**   רוֹצִים   _____
5. **אתה**   **את**   הוֹלֶכֶת   _____

Is the pronoun correct?
Circle yes or no, then write the correct pronoun when needed.

1. הוּא יַלְדָּה.   כן   לא   _____
2. הִיא גָּרָה בְּיִשְׂרָאֵל.   כן   לא   _____
3. הֵם נוֹסְעִים לְאֵילַת.   כן   לא   _____
4. אַתְּ יָכוֹל לִנְסוֹעַ לְחֵיפָה.   כן   לא   _____
5. אַתָּה לוֹמֶדֶת בָּאוּנִיבֶרְסִיטָה.   כן   לא   _____

Second Grammar Break

Here are four forms of the verb, "to want:"

רוֹצוֹת	רוֹצִים	רוֹצָה	רוֹצֶה
female	male	female	male
plural	plural	singular	singular
(f.p.)	(m.p.)	(f.s.)	(m.s.)

Here are four forms of the verb, "to be able:"

יְכוֹלוֹת	יְכוֹלִים	יְכוֹלָה	יָכוֹל
female	male	female	male
plural	plural	singular	singular
(f.p.)	(m.p.)	(f.s.)	(m.s.)

Here are four forms of the verb, "to need:"

צְרִיכוֹת	צְרִיכִים	צְרִיכָה	צָרִיךְ
female	male	female	male
plural	plural	singular	singular
(f.p.)	(m.p.)	(f.s.)	(m.s.)

When we use these three verbs, the following verb will be in the infinitive form. Here are a few examples of infinitives, <u>learn them for future exercises</u>:

to go - לָלֶכֶת	to be - לִהְיוֹת	to speak - לְדַבֵּר
to travel - לִנְסוֹעַ	to visit - לְבַקֵּר	to see - לִרְאוֹת
to eat - לֶאֱכֹל	to work - לַעֲבוֹד	to buy - לִקְנוֹת
to tour - לְטַיֵּל	to sleep - לִישׁוֹן	to do - לַעֲשׂוֹת
to sit - לָשֶׁבֶת	to know - לָדַעַת	to drink - לִשְׁתּוֹת

Here are a few examples: What do they mean in English?

1. אֲנִי צְרִיכָה לָלֶכֶת לְבֵית סֵפֶר.

_____

2. אַתְּ רוֹצָה לִנְסוֹעַ לְתֵל אָבִיב?

_____

3. אֲנַחְנוּ רוֹצִים לֶאֱכֹל פָלָאפֶל.

_____

Create your own sentence, circle the words of your choice:

1. אֲנִי / אַתָּה   צָרִיךְ / צְרִיכָה   לִנְסוֹעַ   לְתֵל אָבִיב / לְאֵילַת.

2. הֵם / הֵן   גָּרִים / גָּרוֹת   בְּאָמֵרִיקָה / בְּיִשְׂרָאֵל.

3. הִיא / הוּא   רוֹצָה / רוֹצֶה   לָלֶכֶת   לִישׁוֹן / לְטַיֵּל.

4. אַתְּ / אַתֶּן   גָּרָה / גָּרוֹת   עַל-יַד   אִמָא / אַבָּא   שֶׁלִי.

Write four sentences in Hebrew,
Use the words "to want" / "to be able" / "to need"

I am a student and I want to visit _____(fill in)_____.

1. _____

I am a boy and I am able to work in the *Kibbutz*.

2. _____

Write two sentences on your own:

3. _____

4. _____

NOTE : The word **אוּנִיבֶרְסִיטָה** is borrowed from English, as is **סְטוּדֶנְט**.
You learned two slang words in this past conversation that are used in the
Hebrew language that are borrowed from Arabic.

hurry up / let's go (Ya'la) - **יָאללָה**   /   awesome (Ah'la) - **אַחְלָה**

Hebrew Quiz:

Ha'Tikva is the National Anthem of Israel.
It was adapted from this poem written by Naftali Herz Imber :

Read the poem in class.

A soul of a Jew still yearns,	כָּל-עוֹד בַּלֵּבָב פְּנִימָה
As long as in his heart within,	נֶפֶשׁ יְהוּדִי הוֹמִיָּה,
And onwards to the ends of the east,	וּלְפַאֲתֵי מִזְרָח קָדִימָה
His eye still looks towards Zion.	עַיִן לְצִיּוֹן צוֹפִיָּה.
*Our hope is not yet lost,	*עוֹד לֹא אָבְדָה תִּקְוָתֵנוּ
The ancient hope:	הַתִּקְוָה הַנּוֹשָׁנָה:
To return to the land of our fathers,	לָשׁוּב לְאֶרֶץ אֲבוֹתֵינוּ,
The city where David encamped.	לָעִיר בָּהּ דָּוִד חָנָה.
As long as tears from our eyes	כָּל-עוֹד דְּמָעוֹת מֵעֵינֵינוּ
Flow like benevolent rain,	יִזְּלוּ כְגֶשֶׁם נְדָבוֹת,
And many of our countrymen	וּרְבָבוֹת מִבְּנֵי עַמֵּנוּ
Still go to the graves of our fathers.*	עוֹד הוֹלְכִים עַל קִבְרֵי אָבוֹת.*
As long as our precious Wall	כָּל-עוֹד חוֹמַת מַחֲמַדֵּינוּ
Appears before our eyes, And	לְעֵינֵינוּ מוֹפָעַת,
And over the destruction of our Temple	וְעַל חֻרְבַּן מִקְדָּשֵׁנוּ
An eye still wells up with tears.*	עַיִן אַחַת עוֹד דּוֹמָעַת.*
As long as the waters of the Jordan	כָּל-עוֹד מֵי הַיַּרְדֵּן בְּגָאוֹן
In fullness swell its banks,	מְלֹא גְדוֹתָיו יִזֹּלוּ,
And down to the Sea of Galilee	וּלְיָם כִּנֶּרֶת בְּשָׁאוֹן
With tumultuous noise fall.*	בְּקוֹל הֲמוּלָה יִפֹּלוּ.*
As long as on the barren highways	כָּל-עוֹד שָׁמָּה עֲלֵי דְרָכַיִם
The humbled city-gates mark,	שַׁעַר יֻכַּת שְׁאִיָּה,
And among the ruins of Jerusalem	וּבֵין חָרְבוֹת יְרוּשָׁלַיִם
A daughter of Zion still cries;*	עוֹד בַּת-צִיּוֹן בּוֹכִיָּה.*

As long as pure tears

from the eye of my nation's daughter flows

To cry for Zion at the watch of night

She still rises in the middle of the nights;*

As long as blood pulses in our veins

it will continue to flow,

And our father's tombs gleam

with the dew that falls; *

As long as the feeling of love of nation

Throbs in the heart of a Jew,

We can still hope even today

That a wrathful God has mercy on us;*

Hear my brothers in the lands of exile,

The one voice of our visionaries,

"Because only with the last Jew,

then there is the end of our hope;"*

כָּל-עוֹד דְּמָעוֹת טְהוֹרוֹת

מֵעֵין בַּת עַמִּי נוֹזְלוֹת,

וְלִבְכּוֹת לְצִיּוֹן בְּרֹאשׁ אַשְׁמוֹרוֹת

עוֹד תָּקוּם בַּחֲצִי הַלֵּילוֹת;*

כָּל-עוֹד נִטְפֵי דָם בְּעוֹרְקֵינוּ

רָצוֹא וָשׁוֹב יִזֹּלוּ,

וַעֲלֵי קִבְרוֹת אֲבוֹתֵינוּ

עוֹד אֶגְלֵי טַל יִפֹּלוּ;*

כָּל עוֹד רֶגֶשׁ אַהֲבַת הַלְאוֹם

בְּלֵב הַיְהוּדִי פּוֹעֵם

עוֹד נוּכַל קַוּוֹת גַּם הַיּוֹם

כִּי עוֹד יְרַחֲמֵנוּ אֵל זוֹעֵם;*

שִׁמְעוּ אַחַי בְּאַרְצוֹת נוּדִי

אֵת קוֹל אַחַד חוֹזֵינוּ

"כִּי רַק עִם אַחֲרוֹן הַיְהוּדִי

גַּם אַחֲרִית תִּקְוָתֵנוּ."*

Here is the final version of the Ha'tikva, the official National Anthem of Israel:

כָּל-עוֹד בַּלֵּבָב פְּנִימָה

נֶפֶשׁ יְהוּדִי הוֹמִיָּה,

וּלְפַאֲתֵי מִזְרָח קָדִימָה

עַיִן לְצִיּוֹן צוֹפִיָּה.

עוֹד לֹא אָבְדָה תִּקְוָתֵנוּ

הַתִּקְוָה בַּת שְׁנוֹת אַלְפַּיִם,

לִהְיוֹת עַם חָפְשִׁי בְּאַרְצֵנוּ

אֶרֶץ צִיּוֹן וִירוּשָׁלַיִם.

Listen to Ha'Tikva

The words are adapted from the poem we just read by Naftali Herz Imber. The music is adapted by Samuel Cohen in 1888 from music by a 16th-century Italian melody, composed by Giuseppe Cenci entitled La Mantovana.

Below is a handwritten verse by Naftali Herz Imber (1878).
Can you recognize some of the words? Notice how the letters are written in print (not script). Circle five words you recognize and write them in script.

_____ 1

_____ 2

_____ 3

_____ 4

_____ 5

http://www.nli-education-uk.org/manuscript-of-hatikvah?lightbox=dataItem-j9wkwi4b1

Listen to Neshama

Listen and discuss:
Neshama Carlebach wrote a new version of the *Ha'tikva*.
She changed it from a Jewish voice to an Israeli
voice to accommodate all the citizens of Israel.

Now it's your turn:
Write a two stanza national anthem for Israel - you can adapt the poem we read or write something completely new. If you need more space, write on a separate piece of paper.

_____   _____

_____   _____

_____   _____

_____   _____

_____   _____

Jerusalem   יְרוּשָׁלַיִם

Jerusalem is the capital of Israel. The city is a vibrant mix of old and new. The entire city is built using Jerusalem stone (a pale limestone) that gives it a golden glow when the sunlight hits it. This is why Jerusalem is known as "Jerusalem of Gold" (יְרוּשָׁלַיִם שֶׁל זָהַב).

The modern city of Jerusalem is divided in two, East Jerusalem and West Jerusalem. East Jerusalem is home to a predominantly Muslim population and West Jerusalem is home to a predominantly Jewish population. The old city (עִיר הָעַתִיקָה) in Jerusalem is divided into four sections - Armenian, Christian, Jewish, and Muslim. Each religion cherishes the old city because it holds a tremendous amount of history to all faiths. The old city is walled and is only one square mile. It is bustling with different languages, mouth-watering foods, handmade wares, souvenirs and rich, deep ties to a time long ago.

5 min history of Jerusalem.

Jerusalem 1911

*The black and white "stamp" seen above is the printers' mark of Marco Antonio Giustiniani (Venice, 1545-52). It was stamped on the title page of the Hebrew books he published and shows the Jewish Temple in Jerusalem depicted as the Dome of the Rock.

שִׂיחָה שֵׁשׁ

הַסְפּוֹרְט

Watch this conversation

יוֹנִית: נוּ[1] אֲרִי! יאללה, עכשיו! מה אתה עושה?

אֲרִי: אני צריך לקנות מַיִם[2] מֵהַשׁוּק[3].

יוֹנִית: אנחנו צריכים להיות בְּמִשְׂחָק[4] עִם הַחֲבֵרִים שֶׁלָנוּ[5].

אֲרִי: אני מוּכָן[6], אני בָּא[7] עכשיו. מָה נִשְׁמַע[8]?

יוֹנִית: הַכָּל[9] בְּסֵדֶר[10]. ואתה?

אֲרִי: הַכָּל טוֹב[11]. לְאָן[12] אנחנו הולכים?

יוֹנִית: אנחנו הולכים לבית הספר, יֵשׁ[13] שָׁם[14] מִגְרָשׁ[15].

אֲרִי: כן, אני מְשַׂחֵק[16] כַּדוּרֶגֶל[17] שָׁם כָּל הַזְמַן[18]. מִפֹּה[19], אנחנו הולכים יָשָׁר[20] ובית הספר בְּצַד[21] יָמִין[22].

יוֹנִית: הַמִגְרָשׁ גָּדוֹל[23]?

אֲרִי: כן, הַמִגְרָשׁ גָּדוֹל. אַתְ רוֹצָה מַיִם? כִּי[24] אֵין[25] מָיִם עַל-יַד הַמִגְרָשׁ.

יוֹנִית: כן, תּוֹדָה.

אֲרִי: בְּבַקָשָׁה[26].

מִלוֹן

14. שָׁם - (over) there		1. נוּ - come on (slang)	
15. מִגְרָשׁ - sport field		2. מַיִם - water	
16. מְשַׂחֵק - play/playing (m.s.)		3. שׁוּק - Shuk (open market)	
17. כַּדוּרֶגֶל - football (soccer)		4. מִשְׂחָק - (a) game	
18. כָּל הַזְמַן - all the time		5. שֶׁלָנוּ - our (ours)	
19. פֹּה - here		6. מוּכָן - ready (m.s.)	
20. יָשָׁר - straight		7. בָּא - coming (m.s.)	
21. בְּצַד - on (the) side		8. מָה נִשְׁמַע* - How are you?	
22. יָמִין - right (direction)		9. הַכָּל - everything (is)	
23. גָדוֹל - big		10. בְּסֵדֶר - okay	
24. כִּי - because		11. טוֹב - good	
25. אֵין - there is not		12. לְאָן - to where	
26. בְּבַקָשָׁה - (you are) welcome, please		13. יֵשׁ - there is/are	

*slang - literally "what's to hear."

Conversation Six
The Sports

Ahdoot (אַחְדוּת) means to join as one. In Israel, this feeling is apparent every day. It is the ethos of the Jewish people. The sports in Israel is one way Jews come together. The Jewish athletic organizations in Israel began before the establishment of the state. Organizations like Hapoel and Maccabi brought athletes together since the early 1900s. Sports in Israel are a large part of the culture and a way to unite the nation.

The first greatest achievement in Israel's sports history was in 1977.

Tal Brody, a Jewish American basketball player who moved to Israel, led his Maccabi team to the European Cup Championship. He took the Israeli basketball team to a new level and put them "On the Map."

Watch a video clip here :

Israelis love Extreme Sports such as:

Skateboarding
Scuba Diving
Surfing
Sky-Diving
Snowboarding and more...

Israeli athletes that have been put on the world stage:

Yael Arad - Judo - 1st Olympic medal for Israel
Gal Fridman - Sailing - Olympic Gold medal
Shahar Pe'er - Tennis - WTA tour
Omri Caspi - Basketball - NBA player
Maccabi Tel Aviv - 6 EuroLeague basketball championships
375 Israelis won medals in the Paralympics.

Shabbat שַׁבָּת - Saturday is the day of rest for the Jewish religion. Because Israel is a Jewish state, many players refuse to play on Saturday because it violates their right to observe שַׁבָּת.

Of course, international games have to be played when scheduled, and players can choose if they want to participate.

In Israel, public transportation does not run on Shabbat and, in many parts of the country, stores are closed. Shabbat is observed from sundown on Friday evening to sundown Saturday evening.

Read an article about it :

Sometimes sports bring Jews and Arabs together. Here is a video of Arab soccer players on an Israeli soccer team :

שִׂיחָה שֵׁש
הַסְפּוֹרְט

Answer these questions in Hebrew:
Use the conversation on page 58.

1. מה אָרִי צָרִיךְ לִקְנוֹת בַּשׁוּק?
_____

_____

2. עִם מִי אָרִי וְיוֹנִית צְרִיכִים לִהְיוֹת?
_____

_____

3. לְאָן אָרִי וְיוֹנִית הוֹלְכִים?
_____

_____

4. הַמִּגְרָשׁ בְּבֵית הַסְפֵר גָדוֹל?
_____

_____

What sports do you like?

_ כַּדּוּרֶגֶל - (Soccer (football

_ כַּדּוּרְסַל - Basketball

_ פּוּטְבּוֹל - American Football

_ בֵּיְסְבּוֹל, כַּדּוּר בָּסִיס - Baseball

_ סַיִף - Fencing

_ כַּדּוּרְעָף - Volleyball

_ גְּלִישָׁה - Surfing

_ גְּלִישַׁת רוּחַ - Windsurfing

_ שְׂחִיָה - Swimming

_ סְקֵייטְבּוֹרְד - Skateboard

_ לִרְכֹּב עַל אוֹפַנַיִם - Ride a bike

_ רִיצָה - Running

_ ג'וּדוֹ - Judo

_ רִיקוּד - Dancing

*כַּדּוּר / כַּדּוּרִים - ball / balls

Draw a picture, or cut and paste a picture, of a sport you like.
If you don't like any sports, you can choose a game or other activity.

Look up two more Hebrew words connected to your chosen sport or game
and share them with your class:

_____ - _____ / _____ - _____

| English | Hebrew | English | Hebrew |

שִׂיחָה שֵׁשׁ

הַסְפּוֹרְט

Learn the word "of":

שֶׁל - of

The word **שֶׁל** can be used alone:

אֵלֶּה הַסְפָרִים שֶׁל בֵּית הַסֵפֶר.

These are the books **of** the school.

Or **שֶׁל** can be used as a contraction:

ours - שֶׁלָנוּ	mine - שֶׁלִי
yours (m.p.) - שֶׁלָכֶם	your (m.s.) - שֶׁלְךָ
yours (f.p.) - שֶׁלָכֶן	your (f.s.) - שֶׁלָךְ
theirs (m.p.) - שֶׁלָהֶם	his - שֶׁלוֹ
theirs (f.p.) - שֶׁלָהֶן	hers - שֶׁלָה

Notice the suffixes. These suffixes will be used with many other contractions:

Here are examples of how it is translated.

Of me or "mine" - שֶׁל אֲנִי = שֶׁלִי

Of you or "your" - שֶׁל אַתָּה = שֶׁלְךָ

Write two sentences using the word "שֶׁל":

_____ .1

_____ .2

Conversation Six
The Sports

Create your own sentence, circle the words of your choice:

1. זֶה / אֵלֶּה סֵפֶר* / סְפָרִים* שֶׁל הַיֶלֶד / הַיַלְדָה.

2. הוּא / הֵם מוּכָן / מוּכָנִים לָלֶכֶת לַשׁוּק / לַמִשְׂחָק.

3. זֶה / זֹאת אִמָּא / אַבָּא שֶׁלִי / שֶׁלוֹ.

4. הִיא / הוּא יָכוֹל / יְכוֹלָה לְשַׂחֵק בַּמִגְרָשׁ שֶׁלָנוּ / שֶׁלָכֶם.

5. אַתְּ / אַתָּה הוֹלֶכֶת / הוֹלֵךְ לַבַּיִת שֶׁלִי / שֶׁלוֹ ?

6. מָה אַתֶּם / אַתֶּן רוֹצִים / רוֹצוֹת לַעֲשׂוֹת הַיּוֹם ?

* סֵפֶר / סְפָרִים - Book / Books

Translate the sentences you created above:

1. _____

2. _____

3. _____

4. _____

5. _____

6. _____

Hebrew
Quiz:

Israel is not necessarily known for its sports, but sports are a big part of Israeli culture. Almost any home you walk into will have a game on TV. Soccer and Basketball are the most popular sports to watch (and play) in Israel. The two oldest sports organizations in Israel are Maccabi and Hapoel. There is also Betar, Elitzur and the ASA (Academic Sports Association).

The Maccabi club is the largest and longest running Jewish sports organization with over 400,000 members. The Maccabi Sports Organization was founded in Tel Aviv in 1912. The Maccabi club hosts the Maccabiah games every four years. The first Maccabiah games were held in 1932 and hosted 390 Jewish athletes from eighteen countries including sixty from Arab lands (Syria and Egypt). The Maccabiah games are also known as the "Jewish Olympics." Today the Maccabi association has over 170 clubs worldwide.

The Hapoel organization is the second largest organization and was established on May 15th, 1926. The logo, painted in red, presents a sportsman inside a sickle and hammer - the slogan is, "Sport for the people and champions." Today Hapoel has over 30 football (soccer) teams, 6 basketball teams and 5 general sports clubs.

Article on sports in Israel:

Images used with permission and in courtesy of Shamir Brothers Studio / Designed by Gabriel and Maxim Shamir.

Conversation Six
The Sports

Research and share: The posters on the previous page were designed by the Shamir Brothers. The Shamir Brothers designed many posters, coins, medals, stamps, banknotes, books and booklets in Israel since the mid-1930s to the early 1990s. Visit their web site and find a poster that catches your eye. Read about it and share your poster and it's significance with your class. You will see that their posters can tell the history of Israel through art and design. If you can, print your posters and have a gallery walk in your classroom of Israel's history through the eyes and designs of the Shamir Brothers. Use the box below to paste a copy of the poster you chose, write the significance of it, and why you chose it. (This project can be on any topic found on their site, not just sports.)

Visit the
Shamir Brothers web site:

If the site comes up in Hebrew, click on the "English" button in the upper left corner of the web site.

If you need more space or if you can create a larger project, use this page to sketch your ideas.
You can work on another piece of paper, on a poster board or on digital media.

שִׂיחָה שֶׁבַע

הָאוֹמָנוּת וְהַתַּרְבּוּת

עֲדִינָה: שלום יָעֵל! מָה נִשְׁמַע?

יָעֵל: הַכֹּל בְּסֵדֶר. לְאָן אנחנו הוֹלְכוֹת[1] הַיּוֹם?

עֲדִינָה: אנחנו הוֹלְכוֹת עִם הֶחָבֵר[2] שלי לטייל בתל אביב.

יָעֵל: אֵיזֶה[3] כֵּיף[4]! שלום, אני יָעֵל. אֵיךְ קוֹרְאִים לְךָ[5]?

לִיאוֹר: שלום אני לִיאוֹר, נעים מאוד. מוּכָנוֹת[6] לָלֶכֶת?

Watch this conversation

יָעֵל: כֵּן, תּוֹדָה.

לִיאוֹר: בְּבַקָּשָׁה. אָז[7], אנחנו הוֹלְכִים מִגְּוֵה צֶדֶק לְכִיכַּר הַבִּימָה.

עֲדִינָה: אַחְלָה!

לִיאוֹר: הִנֵּה[8] מֶרְכַּז[9] סוּזָן דָּלָל. מפֹּה אֲנַחְנוּ הוֹלְכִים יָשָׁר, וּבִרְחוֹב[10] אַהֲרוֹן שָׁלוּשׁ פּוֹנִים[11] שְׂמֹאלָה[12], בִּרְחוֹב שַׁבְּזִי פּוֹנִים יָמִינָה[13], עוֹד פַּעַם[14] יָמִינָה בְּתַחְכְּמוֹנִי וּבְאֶחָד הָעָם פּוֹנִים עוֹד פַּעַם שְׂמֹאלָה. מִשָּׁם הוֹלְכִים יָשָׁר עַד[15] הַסּוֹף[16]. כִּיכַּר הַבִּימָה בְּצַד יָמִין.

יָעֵל: אַחְלָה! אני אוֹהֶבֶת[17] אֶת כִּיכַּר הַבִּימָה, מאוד יפה שם.

לִיאוֹר: בַּדֶּרֶךְ[18] יֵשׁ גָּלֶרְיוֹת שֶׁל אוֹמָנוּת[19], גְּרָפִיטִי עַל הַקִּירוֹת[20], חֲנוּיוֹת[21], מִסְעָדוֹת[22] וְיֵשׁ הַרְבֵּה[23] בָּתֵי קָפֶה[24].

מִלּוֹן

13. יָמִינָה - to the right	1. הוֹלְכוֹת - walk/go (f.p.)
14. עוֹד פַּעַם - one more time	2. חָבֵר - friend (m.s.).
15. עַד - until	3. אֵיזֶה - which
16. סוֹף - end	4. כֵּיף - fun *
17. בַּדֶּרֶךְ - on (in) the way	5. אֵיךְ קוֹרְאִים לְךָ - What's your (m.s.) name**
18. אוֹהֶבֶת - like / love (f.s.)	6. מוּכָנוֹת - ready (f.p.)
19. גָּלֶרְיוֹת שֶׁל אוֹמָנוּת - galleries of art	7. אָז - then, so
20. גְּרָפִיטִי עַל הַקִּירוֹת - graffiti on the walls	8. הִנֵּה - here
21. חֲנוּיוֹת - stores	9. מֶרְכַּז - center
22. מִסְעָדוֹת - restaurants	10. רְחוֹב - street
23. הַרְבֵּה - many (a lot)	11. פּוֹנִים - turning (m.p.)
24. בָּתֵי קָפֶה - coffee houses	12. שְׂמֹאלָה - to the left

*אֵיזֶה כֵּיף translates to "How fun!"   **slang - literally, how do they call you (m.s.)

Conversation Seven
The Arts and Culture

Partial map of

Tel Aviv

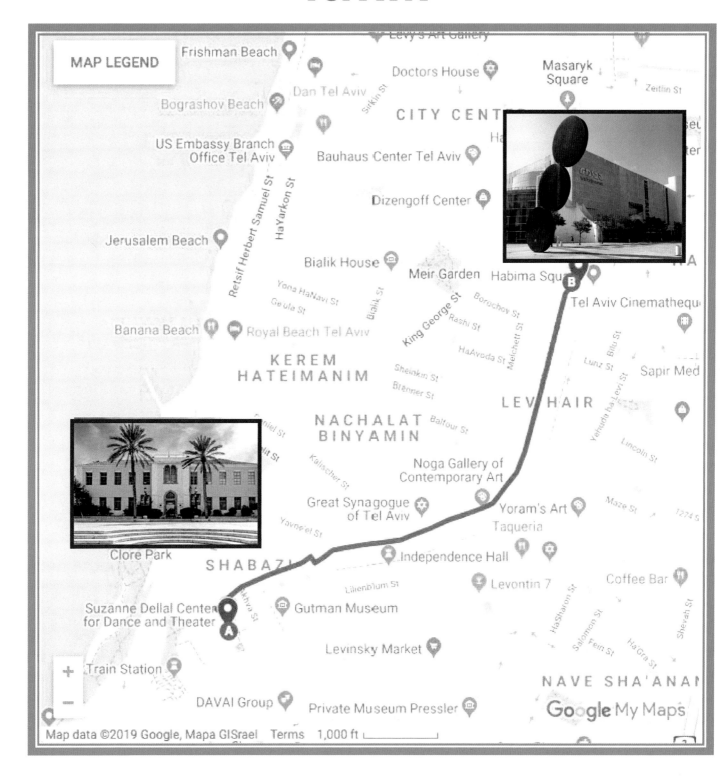

Image courtesy of @winter.of.74

Tel Aviv is the cultural hub of Israel. There are more centers for the performing arts, theaters, dance companies, opera and classical music performances than anywhere else in the country. It is home to Israel's National Theater, *Habima*. *Habima* is committed to the spirit of the Jewish people through the revival of Hebrew culture and language. It was the first theater in the early 1900s to put on performances only in the newly revived Hebrew language and continues this tradition until today. It is the home of the Israeli Philharmonic and has represented Israel in a variety of prestigious theatre festivals around Europe.

The Suzanne Dalal Center is housed in the original building of the first Hebrew school in *Ne've Tzedek* (the first Jewish town outside the walls of Jaffa). It has four performance halls, rehearsal studios, a restaurant and cafe, and wide plazas that host outdoor performances and events. The Suzanne Dalal Center is home to the Batsheva Dance Company, Inbal Dance Theatre and Inbal Pinto and Avshalom Pollak Dance Company. In addition to these world-class theaters, Tel Aviv has many contemporary art galleries, art studios, and graffiti artists who display in studios and on the streets.

Art is not limited to Tel Aviv. Jerusalem is home to the Bezalel Academy of Arts and Design. When Bezalel opened its doors in 1906, it was committed to the revival of the Jewish Nation and the Hebrew language. Bezalel was the first institution to work with designing fonts for the revival of Hebrew and designing posters to promote the new language and the growing country. It was just around the corner from where Eliezer Ben Yehuda lived, and he was no stranger to the institution. Since its opening, all classes have been and are still taught exclusively in Hebrew.

The city of Tzfat is an artist haven in the north of Israel and has also been the center of Kabbalah (Jewish mysticism) since the 16th century. There are many talented artists and smaller art centers throughout Israel.

Conversation Seven
The Arts and Culture

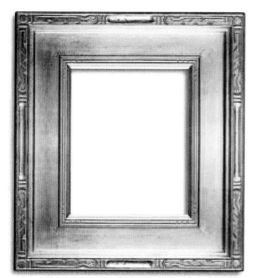

אֲנִי וְחָבֵר שֶׁלִי.

אֲנַחְנוּ פּוֹנִים שְׂמֹאלָה.

אַתָּה גָּר בָּעִיר.

שָׁלוֹם.

אַתֶּן הוֹלְכוֹת לַיָּם.

Two, or more, ways to say it:
Translate to Hebrew.

1. What's your name (m.s.)?_____ or _____

2. How are you (m.s.)?_____ or _____

3. Awesome! _____ or _____

Answer these questions in Hebrew:
Use the conversation on page 66.

1. לְאָן יָעֵל וְעָדִינָה הוֹלְכוֹת?
_____
_____

2. בִּרְחוֹב שַׁבְּזִי פּוֹנִים יָמִינָה אוֹ שְׂמֹאלָה?
_____
_____

3. יָעֵל אוֹהֶבֶת אֶת כִּיכָּר הַבִּימָה?
_____

Connect the best word match:

בְּבֵית סֵפֶר	יֵשׁ
בָּעִיר	תּוֹדָה
בְּבַקָשָׁה	לוֹמְדִים
לְמִסְעָדוֹת	פּוֹנִים
יָמִינָה אוֹ שְׂמֹאלָה	גָּר
לִי	הוֹלְכִים

Match the picture:
Put the number of the word/phrase next to the picture that describes it.
Learn the singular of these words we learned.

1. מִסְעָדוֹת / מִסְעָדָה

2. גְּרָפְטִי עַל הַקִּירוֹת / גְּרָפְטִי עַל הַקִּיר

3. חֲנוּיוֹת / חָנוּת

4. בָּתֵּי קָפֶה / בֵּית קָפֶה

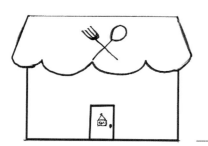   

Write the correct word under the arrow:
Left - Straight - Right

יָמִין - יָשָׁר - שְׂמֹאל

_____   _____   _____

Note that when a direction has a "ח" at the end, it gives it movement.

For example : יָמִין means "right" and יָמִינָה means "to the right."

שִׂיחָה שֶׁבַע

הָאוֹמָנוּת וְהַתַּרְבּוּת

Complete each sentence. Circle the correct word in bold.
Use the map below as your guide.

1. בֵּית הַסֵפֶר בְּצַד **יָמִין / שְׂמֹאל**

2. הַמִּסְעָדָה בְּצַד **יָמִין / שְׂמֹאל**

3. הַחנויות בְּצַד **יָמִין / שְׂמֹאל**

4. בֵּית הַקפה בְּצַד **יָמִין / שְׂמֹאל**

5. מִבֵּית הסֵפר פּוֹנִים **יָמִינָה / שְׂמֹאלָה** לַבֵּית הקפה.

6. מֵהַגלריה פּוֹנִים **יָמִינָה / שְׂמֹאלָה** לַמַּכֹּלֶת

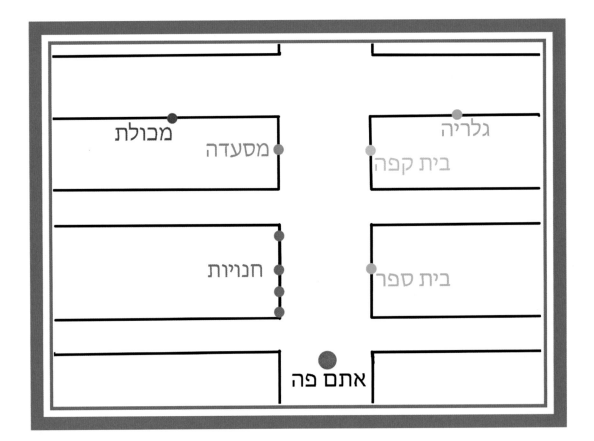

Conversation Seven

The Arts and Culture

Is the statement true? Circle yes or no.

Use the map on the opposite page.

1. הגלריה על-יד החנויות.   כן   לא
2. המסעדה על-יד המכולת.   כן   לא
3. בית הקפה על-יד הגלריה.   כן   לא
4. המסעדה על-יד בית הספר.   כן   לא
5. החנויות על-יד הגלריה.   כן   לא
6. בית הספר על-יד בית הקפה.   כן   לא

Giving directions within a conversation:

Use the words we learned to give directions to a classmate.
Direct them somewhere close to your classroom.

If you want, you can write the directions here:

____

____

____

Hebrew Quiz:

 ©2018 Michelle Geft

Read about a few Israeli artists:

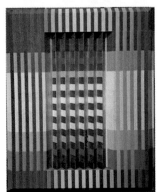

Photo courtesy Anna and Merrit Quarum.

YA'AKOV AGAM

World renown Israeli kinetic artist was born Ya'akov Gipstein in 1928 in Rishon-le-Zion, near Tel Aviv. Agam studied in Jerusalem, Zürich, and Paris. His works are included in the collections of The Museum of Modern Art in New York, the Hirshhorn Museum and Sculpture Garden in Washington D.C., the Santa Barbara Museum of Art, Musée National d'Art Moderne in Paris, and the Solomon R. Guggenheim Museum in New York.

Photo courtesy Murdo MacLeod.

AMOS OZ

Amos Oz was born in Jerusalem in 1939. He was a world renown author of fourteen novels and collections of short fiction, and numerous works of nonfiction. His acclaimed memoir, A Tale of Love and Darkness, was an international bestseller and recipient of the prestigious Goethe prize and National Jewish Book Award. It was also made into a movie starring Natalie Portman.

Image used with permission. Photo Credit : Elad Weissman

IDAN RAICHEL PROJECT

Idan Raichel Project has brought together over eighty artists from all over the world to collaborate through music. Most of the musicians are Israelis with roots in places as diverse as Yemen, Ethiopia, and the former USSR. They have performed all over the world and continue to fuse different sounds and languages. The album "Within My Walls" has songs in Hebrew, Moroccan Arabic, Spanish, Cape Verdean Creole, and Swahili.

Illustration by Avi Katz   avikatz.com

YEHUDA AMICHAI

Yehuda Amichai is one of Israel's leading poets since the mid 1960s. He was born in Germany to a Jewish Orthodox family and moved to pre-state Israel when he was twelve. Amichai's poems have been translated into forty languages, and entire volumes of his work have been published in English, French, German, Swedish, Spanish, and Catalan.

Which artist do you relate to most?

Hear
Ofra Haza

Photo by Nachoom Assis.

OFRA HAZA

Born in Tel Aviv to Yemenite parents is one of Israel's most loved singers. Her songs were top hits in Israel and in Europe. She has collaborated with many artists worldwide. Her song, "Im Nin-alu" sold over two million copies worldwide. She sang Naomi Shemer's song, *Yerushalayim Shel Za'hav"* (Jerusalem of Gold) in 1997 at Israel's 50th anniversary ceremony. This song is considered by many as Israel's second national anthem.

Photo and text used with permission from www.nitzanmintz.com

NITZAN MINTZ

Mintz's work is created in the public sphere, outdoors and between the studio walls, indoors. Her process integrates her poetic work and the material that contains it and their physical, actual location in the street. Her poems combine the personal with the political; they are written out of an internal urge to verbalize mental process which responds to the outside world. The locations she chooses for her work within the urban landscape charges them with social and political meanings.

Explore links
to artists:

From Venezuela by Ohad Naharin (2017). Photo by: Ascaf.
Courtesy Batsheva Dance Company

BATSHEVA DANCE COMPANY

Batsheva Dance Company has been critically acclaimed and popularly embraced as one of the foremost contemporary dance companies in the world. Batsheva Dance Company was founded as a repertory company in 1964 by the Baroness Batsheva de Rothschild who enlisted Martha Graham as its first artistic adviser. Since 1989, Batsheva Dance has been in residence at the Suzanne Dalal Centre in Tel Aviv.

Image courtesy of artist, Hanoch Piven - www. pivenworld.com

ARIK EINSTEIN

Arik Einstein's songs are considered the "Soundtrack of Israel." He was born and raised in Tel Aviv and became an Israeli cultural icon who is thought of as one of the pioneers of Israeli Rock music. He is widely considered to be one of the most influential and prolific Israeli artists of all time. His music will live forever in hearts of Israelis.

Project : Choose or find an Israeli artist and learn more about them. Create a small project that mimics their craft. i.e. If you choose a poet, write a poem.

שִׂיחָה שְׁמוֹנֶה

הָאוֹכֶל

אוֹרְלִי: שלום.

גַּל: שלום, אוֹרְלִי!

אוֹרְלִי: שלום, גַּל. מָתַי[1] אַת יכולה ללכת לַמִּסְעָדָה הַחֲדָשָׁה[2]?

גַּל: אוּלַי[3] השבוע. אנחנו צריכות לְהַזְמִין[4] מָקוֹם[5]?

Watch this conversation

אוֹרְלִי: כן, ואני חוֹשֶׁבֶת[6] שֶׁאֵין[7] מָקוֹם בָּעֶרֶב[8] עד הַחֹדֶשׁ[9] הַבָּא. אז, אַת רוצה בֹּקֶר אוֹ[10] צָהֳרַיִם[11]?

גַּל: אני מַעֲדִיפָה[12] בַּצָּהֳרַיִם, וְאַת?

אוֹרְלִי: כן, גם אני מַעֲדִיפָה בַּצָּהֳרַיִם. איזה יום[13] טוב לָךְ[14]?

גַּל: כָּל יום טוב לי[15] חוּץ[16] מִסּוֹף[17] הַשָּׁבוּעַ[18] וְיוֹם רְבִיעִי[19].

אוֹרְלִי: אוֹקֵי. כל יום טוב לי חוּץ מִיוֹם שִׁישִׁי[20]. אז אני מַזְמִינָה[21] מָקוֹם עכשיו.

גַּל: מְעוּלֶה[22]! תודה. מה אַת עושה היום?

אוֹרְלִי: אני צריכה ללכת לַמַּכֹּלֶת או לַסּוּפֶּר כְּדֵי[23] לִקְנוֹת אוֹכֶל[24]. אֵין לי אוֹכֶל בַּבַּיִת[25]. אַת רוצה לֶאֱכוֹל פֹּה הַלַּיְלָה[26]?

גַּל: כן, תודה!

מִלּוֹן

14. לָךְ – for you, to you (f.s.)		1. מָתַי – when
15. לִי – for me, to me		2. חֲדָשָׁה – new (f.s.)
16. חוּץ – outside of (aside from)		3. אוּלַי – maybe
17. סוֹף – end		4. לְהַזְמִין – to reserve (to invite)
18. שָׁבוּעַ – week		5. מָקוֹם – place
19. יוֹם רְבִיעִי – Wednesday		6. חוֹשֶׁבֶת – think (f.s)
20. יוֹם שִׁישִׁי – Friday		7. שֶׁ... – that...
21. מַזְמִינָה – order/reserve (f.s.)		8. עֶרֶב – evening
22. מְעוּלֶה – awesome		9. חֹדֶשׁ – month
23. כְּדֵי – in order to		10. אוֹ – or
24. אוֹכֶל – food		11. צָהֳרַיִם – afternoon
25. בַּיִת – home / house		12. מַעֲדִיפָה – prefer (f.s.)
26. לַיְלָה – night		13. יוֹם – day

SHWARMA KEBAB LAFFAH ISRAELI SALAD

FALAFEL HUMMUS TEHINA SHAKSHUKA

Watch a short video on street food in Israel:

Answer these questions in Hebrew:
Use the conversation on page 76.

1. ‏לאן אוֹרְלִי וְגַל רוצות ללכת?

_____

2. ‏מָתַי גַל מַעֲדִיפָה ללכת?

_____

3. ‏מי מזמינה מקום?

_____

4. ‏מה אוֹרְלִי צריכה לעשות היום?

_____

Combining words we learned to make everyday phrases:

On page 38 we learned the Hebrew word טוֹב means "good."

In this conversation we learned (Fill in the English):

לַיְלָה	עֶרֶב	יוֹם	בּוֹקֶר
_____	_____	_____	_____

We can combine words we learned to form common, everyday phrases:

Good morning	-	בּוֹקֶר טוֹב
Good day	-	יוֹם טוֹב
Good evening	-	עֶרֶב טוֹב
Good night	-	לַיְלָה טוֹב

Conversation Eight
The Food

What day of the week do you like to eat out?

Sunday.............................יוֹם רִאשׁוֹן

Monday............................יוֹם שֵׁנִי

Tuesday.........................יוֹם שְׁלִישִׁי

Wednesday....................יוֹם רְבִיעִי

Thursday.......................יוֹם חֲמִישִׁי

Friday............................יוֹם שִׁשִׁי

Sabbath (Saturday)..........יוֹם שַׁבָּת

אֵיזֶה יוֹם הַיוֹם?
_____

אֵיזֶה יוֹם יִהְיֶה* מָחָר*?
_____

אֵיזֶה יוֹם הָיָה* אֶתְמוֹל*?
_____

אֵיזֶה יָמִים הֵם סוֹף הַשָׁבוּעַ שֶׁלָכֶם?
_____

* יִהְיֶה - will be   מָחָר - tomorrow   הָיָה - was   אֶתְמוֹל - yesterday

Did you know?
In Israel, Sunday through Thursday are work and school days.
The official weekend is Friday and Saturday.

In Chapter 6, we learned the words יֵשׁ / אֵין
Let's review these words and learn how to use them in context.

There is - יֵשׁ

There isn't - אֵין

יש מִגְרָשׁ שָׁם?

לַמּוֹרָה יש סְפָרִים.

יש לְמִסְעָדָה תַּפְרִיט?

אין סְטוּדֶנְטִים בבית ספר בְּיוֹם שִׁישִׁי.

אין אוֹכֶל בַּבַּיִת שֶׁל אוֹרְלִי.

****

In Hebrew, it is common to use the adverb "to" with יֵשׁ / אֵין.
He are popular conjugations to use with these words:

לְ... - to

to us - לָנוּ	to me - לִי
to you (m.p.) - לָכֶם	to you (m.s.) - לְךָ
to you (f.p.) - לָכֶן	to you (f.s.) - לָךְ
to them (m.p.) - לָהֶם	to him - לוֹ
to them (f.p.) - לָהֶן	to her - לָהּ

Here are examples of how it is translated:

There is to me or "I have" - יֵשׁ לִי

There is not to us or "we do not have" - אֵין לָנוּ

(Notice the suffixes of the words above are the same as the words for שֶׁל on page 62.)

Translate to English:

1. יֵשׁ לָהּ סְפָרִים. _____

2. יֵשׁ לָכֶן תַּפְרִיט? _____

3. אֵין לָנוּ בֵּית סֵפֶר בְּיוֹם שִׁישִׁי. _____

_____

4. אֵין לִי אוֹכֶל בַּבַּיִת. _____

Create your own sentences. Circle the words of your choice:

1. יֵשׁ / אֵין   לָהּ / לוֹ   כֶּסֶף* / אוֹכֶל.

2. יֵשׁ / אֵין   לַבֵּית סֵפֶר   מִגְרָשׁ / בְּרֵיכָה**.

3. בְּיוֹם שִׁישִׁי יֵשׁ / אֵין   לָהֶם / לָכֶם   מָקוֹם בַּבַּיִת שֶׁלָהֶם / שֶׁלָכֶם
לְתַלְמִידִים / לְאוֹרְחִים.***

4. יֵשׁ / אֵין   עִיר / קִיבּוּץ   בַּדֶרֶךְ   לְתֵל אָבִיב / לְחֵיפָה?

5. יֵשׁ / אֵין   חֲנוּיוֹת / גָלֵרִיוֹת   בְּאֵירוֹפָה / בְּאַרְצוֹת הַבְּרִית.

guests - אוֹרְחִים***   pool - בְּרֵיכָה**   money - כֶּסֶף*

Translate the sentences you created above:

1. _____

2. _____

3. _____

4. _____

5. _____

שִׂיחָה שְׁמוֹנֶה

הָאוֹכֶל

1. מתי אתה/את מעדיף/מעדיפה ללכת למסעדה? _____

_____

2. עם מי אתה/את רוצה ללכת למסעדה? _____

_____

3. איזה אוכל אתה/את אוהב/אוהבת לאכול ? _____

_____

4. את/אתה רוצה לאכול בקיבוץ? למה או למה לא? _____

_____

5. איזה שפה את/אתה מדבר/מדברת? _____

_____

6. איפה אתה/את גר/גרה ? _____

_____

7. מה אתה/את עושה בשבוע הבא? _____

_____

8. אתה/את אוהב/אוהבת ללמוד עברית? למה או למה לא? _____

_____

_____

9. על-יד מי אתה/את רוצה לשבת? _____

_____

Conversation Eight
The Food

_____

_____

_____

_____

_____

_____

_____

_____

_____

_____

_____

_____

Hebrew
Quiz:

שִׂיחָה שְׁמוֹנֶה
הָאוֹכֶל

Israeli cuisine is a mosaic of foods that integrates the palettes of immigrant Jews mostly from the Middle East and Arab lands.

Falafel - Some believe that falafel most likely originated in Egypt, where it is called ta'amiya and is made from fava beans (though others claim it comes from India). Falafel was made popular in Israel by Yemenite Jews in the 1950s. They brought with them the chickpea version of the dish from Yemen and introduced the concept of serving falafel balls in pita bread. There is controversy over who "invented" the falafel but it has become a staple in Israeli food nevertheless.

Shawarma - Shawarma is thought to have become popular during the Ottoman Empire and may have originated in Turkey. Shawarma consists of pieces of spiced meat piled on a spit. It slowly roasts as it rotates for hours. The word "shawarma" derives from a Turkish word that means "turning." It is typically made from veal, but you can find beef, chicken and turkey shawarma as well.

Shakshuka - Brought to Israel by Jewish immigrants from North Africa (some think from Yemen), this dish consists of poached eggs cooked in spiced stewed tomatoes. It is served at breakfast but can be eaten at any time of the day.

Israeli Salad - The Israeli salad is a staple in the Mediterranean diet - it can be served at any meal. This salad is made of a base of finely chopped tomatoes, cucumbers, onion, olive oil and lemon juice. Favorite additions are parsley and feta cheese.

Hummus - Hummus is made almost entirely of cooked and mashed chickpeas with garlic, lemon juice, olive oil, salt and some add tehina. The origin of Hummus is highly contested but there is evidence that chickpeas have been around for human consumption for several thousands of years and the true origins cannot be pinpointed (as most of the foods on this list). It is thought that the Hummus dip we enjoy today may have its origins in Egypt in the 13th century.

Tahina - Tahina, or "tahini," is ground sesame seeds. Sesame seeds have been cultivated in India since 5000 BC, and there are references to it found in Mesopotamia. The most recent history is unknown, but in Israel, it is prepared with garlic, lemon, and salt. It is usually served with Hummus, but it is also used as a dip and a dressing for many different foods.

Kebob - Many say that it originated in Turkey by the Turkish soldiers who cooked their hunted meat on their swords, turning it over an open fire. Kebab is now a world-wide food. In America, we make skewers on our bar-b-que, which are a version of Kebab. In Asia, they make satay, In Nepal, it is Sekuwa and in West Africa it is Suya. There are many versions of Kebob around the world.

Sabich - A sandwich that was originally made with hard boiled egg, Israeli salad, amba, and fried eggplant in a pita. It is named after Sabich Zvi Halabi, an Iraqi Jew who immigrated to Israel in the 1950s, and created the popular sandwich.

Pita - This bread pocket is made from flour, yeast, warm water, salt, oil. It's origins took place in Mesopotamia over 4000 years ago. Bedouins are believed to have spread the use of the pita into the broader area. Pita is famous around the world and is a staple in the Middle East.

Laffah - Laffah is similar to pita but a little chewier and has no pocket, it's also much larger. It is usually used to wrap meats like shawarma and kebab.

Burekas - A savory stuffed pastry that was brought to Israel by Sephardic immigrants. They are usually stuffed with cheeses, spinach, potatoes and/or meats. Burekas are thought to have originated in Turkey.

Conversation Eight
The Food

Find a recipe online of an Israeli food to share with the class.
If your classroom arrangement allows for it,
make an Israeli feast (or order in)!

Food_____

Recipe:

Picture:

Ingredients needed:

Directions:

Link to find
some recipes :

שִׂיחָה תֵּשַׁע
מֵאַרְכִיאוֹלוֹגְיָה לְטֶכְנוֹלוֹגְיָה

Watch this conversation

גִיל: שלום עֶנְבָּל, מה נשמע?

עֶנְבָּל: הכֹּל בסדר. מה עושים היום?

אָרִי: אנחנו הולכים לַשִׁיעוּר[1].

דָלְיָה: איפה הַשִׁיעוּר?

אָרִי: הַשִׁיעוּר במרכז העיר בירושלים.

גִיל: אנחנו לא מפֹּה. אתה יכול לִשְׁלוֹח[2] לי ס.מ.ס[3] עם הַכְּתוֹבֶת[4].

אָרִי: בָּרוּר[5], אֶפְשָׁר[6] לָשִׂים[7] בְּוֵייז[8].

גִיל: כֵּן, תודה.

אָרִי: הַשִׁיעוּר בְּקוֹמָה[9] שְׁתַּיִם[10], בְּחֶדֶר[11] מִסְפָּר[12] אַרְבַּע[13].

עֶנְבָּל: תודה, ארי. וְכַמָּה[14] שָׁעוֹת[15] הַשִׁיעוּר?

אָרִי: הַשִׁיעוּר מִתֵּשַׁע[16] בַּבֹּקֶר עד שָׁלוֹש[17] בַּצָהֳרַיִם. יש הַפְסָקָה[18] שֶׁל שָׁעָה[19] אַחַת[20] בָּאֶמְצַע[21].

עֶנְבָּל: אַז שֵׁש[22] שָׁעוֹת. אוֹקֵי.

דָלְיָה: עַל[23] מה הַשִׁיעוּר?

גִיל: הַשִׁיעוּר על ארץ ישראל מִזְמַן[24] הַתּוֹרָה וְעַד הַיוֹם.

דָלְיָה: מְעַנְיֵין[25]! אני אוהבת לִלְמוֹד על הָהִסְטוֹרְיָה[26] שֶׁל ישראל.

אָרִי: אני גם אוֹהֵב[27] לִלְמוֹד עַל הָהִסְטוֹרְיָה שֶׁל ישראל. לְהִתְרָאוֹת שָׁם.

גִיל, דָלְיָה, עֶנְבָּל: לְהִתְרָאוֹת!

Explore the Dead Sea scrolls

Photo used with permission and in courtesy of Joshua Cahn @joshtravelstheworld

מִלּוֹן

15. שָׁעוֹת - hours	1. שִׁיעוּר - lesson
16. תֵּשַׁע - nine	2. לִשְׁלוֹחַ - to send
17. שָׁלוֹשׁ - three	3. ס.מ.ס. - s.m.s. (text)
18. הַפְסָקָה - break, recess	4. כְּתוֹבֶת - address
19. שָׁעָה - (an) hour	5. בָּרוּר - of course
20. אַחַת - one	6. אֶפְשָׁר - possible
21. בָּאֶמְצַע - in the middle	7. לָשִׂים - to put
22. שֵׁשׁ - six	8. וֵייז - WAZE
23. עַל - on / about	9. קוֹמָה - floor (story, level)
24. זְמַן - time	10. שְׁתַּיִם - two
25. מְעַנְיֵן - interesting	11. חֶדֶר - room
26. הִסְטוֹרְיָה - history	12. מִסְפָּר - number
27. אוֹהֵב - like / love (m.s.)	13. אַרְבַּע - four
	14. כַּמָּה - how many (much)

The Technion in Haifa is the "M.I.T. of Israel." It opened in 1923. Albert Einstein was a founding supporter and planted a ceremonious tree which still stands today.

Video & info on the Technion

Photo courtesy of Idan Chazan.

Answer these questions in Hebrew:
Use the conversation on page 86.

1. אֵיפֹה הַשִׁיעוּר?

_____

2. מִי הוֹלֵךְ לַשִׁיעוּר?

_____

3. כָּמָה שָׁעוֹת הַשִׁיעוּר?

_____

4. עַל מָה הַשִׁיעוּר?

_____

Choose the appropriate pronoun, then translate:

הוֹלֵךְ	הוּא	הִיא	1.
חוֹשֵׁב	אַתָּה	אַת	2.
גָרוֹת	אַתֵן	אַתֶם	3.
מוּכָנוֹת	הֵן	הֵם	4.
עוֹשָׂה	הִיא	הוּא	5.
פּוֹנִים	הֵם	הֵן	6.
יְכוֹלָה	אַת	אַתָּה	7.
מְדַבֵּר	הוּא	הִיא	8.
עוֹבֵד	אַת	אַתָּה	9.

Learning to count:

אַחַת (1), שְׁתַּיִם (2), שָׁלוֹשׁ (3), אַרְבַּע (4), חָמֵשׁ (5), שֵׁשׁ (6)
שֶׁבַע (7), שְׁמוֹנֶה (8), תֵּשַׁע (9), עֶשֶׂר (10)

Practice counting with your classmate.

In Hebrew, write the number represented:

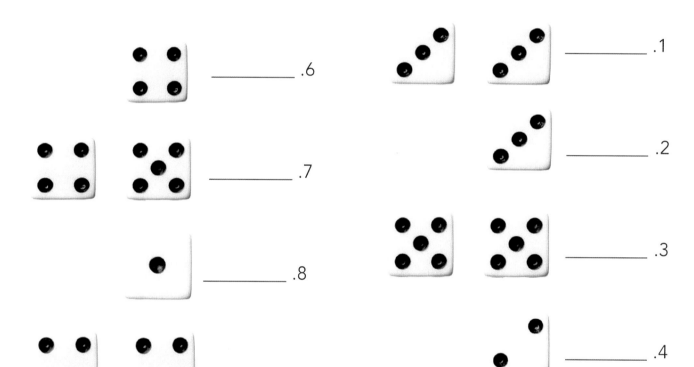

_____ .6

_____ .7

_____ .8

_____ .9

_____ .10

_____ .1

_____ .2

_____ .3

_____ .4

_____ .5

In Israel and throughout the Middle-East,
Backgammon is a very popular board-game
that uses dice. In Hebrew, it is called  שֵׁשׁ בֵּשׁ.

Crossword Puzzle

Review the words you learned.

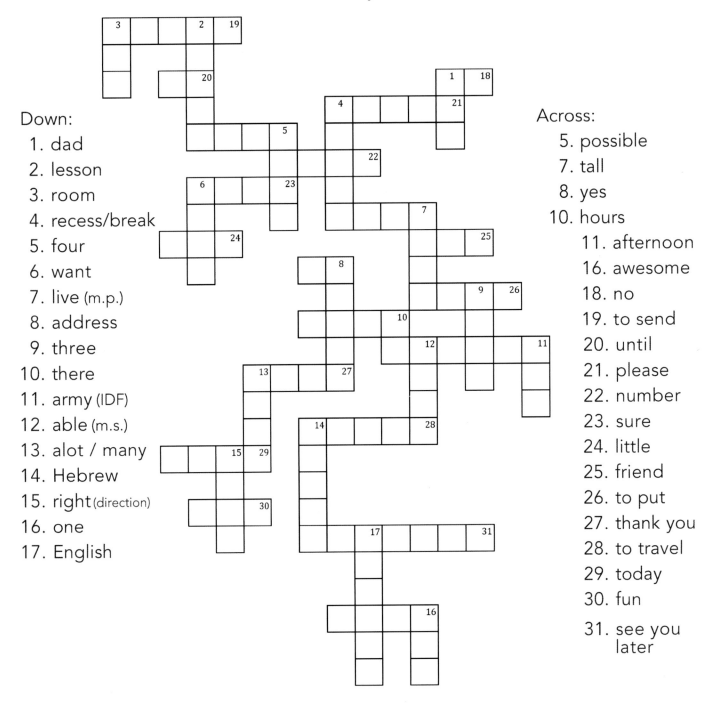

Down:

1. dad
2. lesson
3. room
4. recess/break
5. four
6. want
7. live (m.p.)
8. address
9. three
10. there
11. army (IDF)
12. able (m.s.)
13. alot / many
14. Hebrew
15. right (direction)
16. one
17. English

Across:

5. possible
7. tall
8. yes
10. hours
11. afternoon
16. awesome
18. no
19. to send
20. until
21. please
22. number
23. sure
24. little
25. friend
26. to put
27. thank you
28. to travel
29. today
30. fun
31. see you later

Third Grammar Break

Most of the Hebrew language is built on three letter root-words. These root words are used for building verbs and nouns. Here is an example:

The root word **ל.מ.ד.** which means "learn."

In simple verb form, as you learned on page 34, it looks like this :

לוֹמְדוֹת   לוֹמְדִים   לוֹמֶדֶת   לוֹמֵד

male singular (m.s.)	female singular (f.s.)	male plural (m.p.)	female plural (f.p.)

In a derivative noun form, the root looks like this and means student :

תַּלְמִדוֹת   תַּלְמִידִים   תַּלְמִידָה   תַּלְמִיד

male singular (m.s.)	female singular (f.s.)	male plural (m.p.)	female plural (f.p.)

(This is a synonym to the word סטודנט. Although סטודנט is commonly used for university students, and תלמיד is commonly used for grade school students.)

Other words that derive from the root **ל.מ.ד.** are :

to learn - לִלְמוֹד   to teach - לְלַמֵּד   learnings (of) - לִימוּד

Talmud* - תַּלְמוּד   teaches (m.s.) - מְלַמֵּד   learning - לְמִידָה

Highlight the root letters in all the words on this page.

*Book of Jewish Studies and Law

Why do you think the word for "student" comes from the same root as to "learn"?

_____

_____

Why do you think the word for "teach" comes from the same root as to "learn"?

_____

_____

Find the common root from these words:

Highlight the root letters in the word, then write the root on the left.
Hint: find the three letters that are common in every word.

1. שְׁמוּעָה שׁוֹמֵעַ נִשְׁמָע הַשְׁמָעָה לִשְׁמוֹעַ   ___ · ___ · ___

2. דִּבּוּר מְדַבֵּר לְדַבֵּר דִּבֵּר דִּבָּר   ___ · ___ · ___

3. לְטַיֵּל טִיּוּל טַיֶּלֶת מְטַיֵּל טִיֵּל   ___ · ___ · ___

4. נְסִיעָה נוֹסֵעַ לִנְסוֹעַ נוֹסַעַת נוֹסְעִים   ___ · ___ · ___

5. חוֹשֵׁב חֲשִׁיבָה חָשׁוּב חִישׁוּב הִתְחַשְׁבוּת   ___ · ___ · ___

Use the dictionary in the back of this book and look up the words above.
Can you see the similarities in the definitions? How do the words relate?

Conversation Nine
From the Archaeology to the Technology

Create your own sentence, circle the words of your choice:

1. אֲנִי / אַתה רוֹצֶה / רוֹצָה לָלֶכֶת לַחֲנוּת / לְבֵית קָפֶה.

2. הֵם / הֵן מוּכָנוֹת / מוּכָנִים לִנְסוֹע לִבְאֵר שֶׁבַע / לְאֵילַת.

3. הַמּוֹרָה / הַמּוֹרֶה מְלַמֶּדֶת / מְלַמֵּד עברית / אנגלית.

4. דָלְיָה / אֲרִי לוֹמֵד / לוֹמֶדֶת בְּבֵית סֵפֶר / בְּאוּנִיבֶרְסִיטָה.

5. אתם / אתן פוֹנִים / פוֹנוֹת יָמִינה / שמאלה לגלריה / לחנות.

Write a conversation using the words you learned :

אִיתַי: _____

לֵילָךְ: _____

אִיתַי: _____

לֵילָךְ: _____

אִיתַי: _____

לֵילָךְ: _____

Share your conversation with your classmate. On a separate piece
of paper, write a conversation together then read it for your class.

Hebrew
Quiz:

People relate to Israel in different ways. It is the ancient land of the Israelites and a modern Mediterranean start-up nation. Whether you are interested in history or modernity, Israel has something to offer. Israel has a plethora of historical sites and is at the forefront of many discoveries and innovations. It is an archaeologist's playground and a technology fiend's amusement park. There are hundreds of excavation sites in the 8600 square mile country and, at the same time, hundreds of start-up companies.

Several major discoveries have impacted the world forum and many affected Biblical accounts. The Dead Sea Scrolls that were discovered in Israel in 1946 are considered the most important archaeological find of the twentieth century. They were discovered in the Qumran caves, in Israel's desert, near the Dead Sea. In 2018 human teeth were found in a cave near Tel Aviv. They are dated to be about 180,000 years old. This discovery has changed our idea of human evolution because the oldest human discovery outside Africa dates 60,000 years earlier than this. We now see that humans interacted outside of Africa much earlier than previously thought. In the City of David in Jerusalem, the constant discoveries give us knowledge of what our world looked like hundreds and even thousands of years ago.

Several major innovations have changed the modern world forum. Israel is known as "The Start-Up Nation." Thousands of innovations have come out of Israel, and it is now a hub for many of the major technology companies including IBM, Apple, Google, Intel and more. Most of the technology you are using today has come out of Israel: Intel processors, which can be found in about 80 percent of the world's computers, SD cards, WAZE, heart monitors in watches, many mobile cameras, most of the new iPhone hardware, water purifiers, agricultural advances, military technologies and so much more. The resurrection of the spoken Hebrew language, the founding of the state, the kibbutz, and the I.D.F. are all major successes that came out of this pioneering spirit. This spirit is the foundation to the start-up mentality in Israel. The authors of the book "Start-Up Nation" call Israelis "dissatisfied." This dissatisfaction drives success. The founding of the State of Israel is essentially Israel's first start-up.

Let's explore some of these discoveries and innovations:

Partial list of discoveries:

- Dead Sea Scrolls
- Caesaria - city, mosaic floors and more
- Masada - fortress city on mountain top
- Synagogues with mosaic floor in Galilee
- Synagogues with mosaic floor in Negev
- Tel Arad
- Philistine cemetery near Ashkelon
- City of David
- Beth Alpha mosaic
- Oldest Hebrew writings in Kirbet Qeiyafa
- Gezer Calendar (10th century BCE)
- Gabriel's Revelation
- 2000 year old caves in Galilee
- Gold and Silver items with figurines found in Gezer (3600 years old)
- 7 C.E., 827-square-meter mosaic found in Jericho
- Resistance in Jaffa 12 C.E.
- Tel Megiddo
- Beit She'an
- Roman theater uncovered 1700 years old
- 2000 year old stone workshop in Reina
- Tel Be'er Sheva
- Mamshit
- and so many more...

Partial list of innovations:

- WAZE
- USB drives
- Wireless charging
- Some of Intel's processors
- Israel helped develop the cell phone
- Technologies in Xbox, PS3 and Kindle
- Online messaging developed in Israel
- Answers.com
- Babylon (translating sites)
- Drip irrigation
- Solar Technology
- Desalination (water)
- Alternative fuels
- Mobile eye
- Soda Stream
- Sambucol
- MS treatments
- ADHD treatments
- Depression treatments
- Alzheimer's treatments
- Baby monitor (under mattress)
- Asthma treatments
- Heart attack prevention
- Bandages that helps stop bleeding
- and so many more....

Visit Israel21c.org and nocamels.com for up-to-date innovations from Israel.

Image used with permission from Eilat Mazar.
Photo credit: Ouria Tadmor

Seal of the Prophet Isaiah

This is a 2,700-year-old clay seal impression which potentially belonged to the biblical prophet Isaiah. There is skepticism about the seal itself, but the dating is accurate and parallels nearby archaeological findings. This was found in the City of David in 2018 near other antiquities of the same era.

Image courtesy of Ehud Galili.

Gold coins found off Acre harbor

In 2017, Israeli marine archaeologists found hoards of gold coins from a 13th-century crusader ship. The gold coins sank with the ship in Acre harbor when the Muslims came to take over the Crusaders. The Crusader shipwreck dates to 1062-1250 C.E. Ceramic jugs and bowls imported from Cyprus, Syria, and Italy were also found.

Synagogue floor in the Galilee

Image use and reproduction in courtesy of Jodi Magness.
Photo credit: Jim Haberman

In 2012, mosaics were found in an ancient synagogue in the northern part of Israel. It was excavated in Huqoq, an ancient Jewish village in the country's Galilee region, and dates to the fourth and fifth centuries. The mosaic includes images of women, as well as other biblical scenes. This is an example of very high-quality artwork using tiny colored stones to build this significant mosaic.
http://huqoq.web.unc.edu/

Use the links to explore archaeological sites and new technology in Israel. Choose something that interests you to research and present information about it to your classmates.

A list of archaeological sites in Israel you can explore

Courtesy of Medtronic © 2018

Image used with permission and in courtesy of Rewalk Robotics

Israel technology company GIVEN created a pill in 2001 that is taken by the mouth and takes video of the entire digestive tract. Before the PillCam, doctors had to use invasive procedures to get the same results. PillCam advances global health with less-invasive screening that can improve patient outcomes and lower healthcare costs. It is now widely used by 1.5 million users in 75 countries worldwide.

ReWalk

Israeli developers created an exoskeleton system that enables paralyzed people to walk again. ReWalk allows independent, controlled walking similar to that of a non-disabled person, as computers and motion sensors do the work. There are over 1000 users worldwide. www.rewalk.com

10min video on Israel as a start-up nation

Image used with permission from David Zarrouk

List of up-to-date start-ups in Israel for you to explore

RSTAR, "Rising" Sprawl-Tuned Autonomous Robot

This robot was designed by David Zarrouk, who has his laboratory at the Ben-Gurion University of the Negev. RSTAR is made to handle all terrains such as gravel, stones, grass, and mud. It can also climb vertically and through narrow gaps. RSTAR is suitable for search and rescue operations, even in dangerous, unstable environments.

Visit Israel21c.org and nocamels.com for up-to-date innovations from Israel.

חֲבָל עַל הַזְּמַן

This phrase translates to "shame on the time." It is used when referring to an amazing experience. It is like saying you could only wish for more time.

אֲנִי מֵתָה עָלֶיךָ

Similar to "I die for you," it means "I'm crazy about you".

תִּתְחַדְּשִׁי

This word translates to "be new." It is used when someone purchases new clothing or has a new item. It is like saying "Enjoy your new thing."

חֻצְפָּה

A characteristic trait to describe someone with audacity, be it for good or bad. Now more commonly used to describe someone when they have crossed the line of acceptable behavior.

סְתָם

The word can be used in several ways. It can be used when you do something "just because," or for "no reason."   It is for when something isn't very important.

נְשָׁמָה

A word used similarly to "sweetie" but it literally means "soul." People say "neshama sheli" which means "my soul." It is used often to both men and women. It is like saying you are so important to me that you are part of my soul.

חַי בְּסֶרֶט

Translates to "Living in a movie." When someone is being over the top and unrealistic about a situation.

עַל הַפָּנִים

Translates to "on the face." Used to describe when something was really awful. "The food tonight was on my face," meaning very bad.

סוֹף הַדֶּרֶךְ

Literally means "end of the road," but used to describe something awesome. Like, "that party was *end of the road*."

כַּפָּרָה עָלֶיךָ

The exact translation is "Atonement over you" but used as "darling" or "sweetie." The word Kapara is actually the word used for an old ritual orthodox Jews do on Yom Kippur (the day of atonement).

גַּג

Means "roof." You use it instead of using the word "maximum."

"The Jewish Holiday Song"

To the tune of "It's a Small World" by The Sherman Brothers
Song lyrics copywritten by Michelle Geft

CHORUS:
*These are the Jewish holidays,
We celebrate in so many ways,
Coming together to sing and praise
It's the Jewish Year
Rosh Hashana, is the New Year
Apples n' honey, the shofar we hear,
Yom Kippur is the holiest day
ask forgiveness and Kol Nidre,
We build a Sukkah on Sukkot
schah on the roof, lulav n' etrog,
Simchat Torah five books we complete
dancing, singing in the street.
CHORUS*

Hanukah it lasts eight nights,
spin the dreidel, menorah we light,
Tu B'shvat is the birthday of the trees
come and plant oh won't you please,
On Purim we read Megilat Esther,
wear costumes, Haman we can't bear,
Pesach Seder and Ma' nishtana
we left Egypt eating Matzah.
CHORUS*

Yom Hazikaron we appreciate
the soldiers that fought for our Jewish State
Yom Ha'atzma'ut we raise our flag and tell
the story of Medinat Yisrael
Lag Ba'omer a bonfire we light
Shavuot, got the Torah, HAR SINAI!
Tish'a b'Av is a very sad day
Temples destroyed to our dismay
CHORUS*

But perhaps our most special holiday
is the one that comes every week, hooray!
It's a family time with Challah and wine
and it starts on Friday night.
"Shabbat Shalom" is what we say
we see each other throughout the day
A day of peace and a day of rest
so that everyone feels blessed.
CHORUS*

Listen and watch
video here:

א

Hebrew	Page	English
אַבָּא	46	dad / father
אֲבָל	38	but
אוֹ	76	or
אוֹהֵב	86	like/love (m.s.)
אוֹהֶבֶת	66	like/love (f.s.)
אוֹהֲבוֹת		like/love (f.p.)
אוֹהֲבִים		like/love (m.p.)
אוֹכֶל	76	food
אוּלַי	76	maybe
אוֹמָנוּת	66	art
אוּנִיבֶרְסִיטָה	30	university
אוֹרֵחַ		guest
אוֹרְחִים	81	guests
אָז	68	so
אָח	46	brother
אָחוֹת	46	sister
אֲחָיוֹת	46	sisters
אַחִים		brothers
אַחְלָה	46	awesome
אַחַת	86	one
אֵיזֶה	66	which
אֵיךְ	66	how
אֵיךְ קוֹרְאִים לְךָ	66	What's your name (m.s.)
אֵיךְ קוֹרְאִים לָךְ		What's your name (f.s.)
אֵין	58	there is not
אֵיפֹה	22	where
אֵירוֹפָּה	22	Europe
אֵלֶה	34	these
אִמָא	46	mom/mother
אַנְגְלִית	22	English
אֲנַחְנוּ	38	we
אֲנִי	14	I (am)
אֶפְשָר	86	possible
אַרְבַּע	86	four
אַרְצוֹת הַבְּרִית	46	United States
אַתְּ	14	you (f.s.)
אַתָּה	14	you (m.s.)
אַתֶּם	38	you (m.p.)
אֶתְמוֹל	79	yesterday
אַתֶּן	40	you (f.p.)

ב

Hebrew	Page	English
בְּ...	22	in
בַּ... / בָּ...	38	in the
בָּא	58	comes /coming (m.s.)
בָּאֶמְצַע	86	in the middle
בְּבַקָשָה	58	(you're) welcome, please
בַּדֶּרֶךְ	66	on the way
בְּחֶדֶר	86	in room
בַּיִת	76	home/house
בֵּית סֵפֶר	30	school
בֵּית קָפֶה	69	coffee house
בִּנְיָן	86	building
בְּסֵדֶר	58	okay
בְּצַד	58	on (the) side
בֹּקֶר	38	morning
בֹּקֶר טוֹב	38	good morning
בָּרוּר	86	of course , it is clear
בְּרֵיכָה	81	pool
בָּתֵי קָפֶה	66	coffee houses

ג

Hebrew	Page	English
גָּבוֹהַ	86	tall
גָּדוֹל	58	big
ג'וּדוֹ	**60**	**Judo**
גְּלִישָה	**60**	**Surfing**
גְּלִישַת רוּחַ	60	Windsurfing
גָּלֵרְיָה	72	gallery

Dictionary

Hebrew	English	Page
גַּלֵרִיּוֹת	galleries	66
גָּלֵרִיּוֹת שֶׁל אוֹמָנוּת	art galleries	66
גַּם	also	22
גָּר	live (m.s.)	22
גָּרָה	live (f.s.)	22
גָּרוֹת	live (f.p.)	46
גָּרִים	live (m.p.)	46
גְּרָפִיטִי	graffiti	66
גְּרָפִיטִי עַל הַקִּירוֹת	graffiti on the walls	66

ד

Hebrew	English	Page
דֶּרֶךְ	way	66
דִּבּוּר	speach	92
דִּבֵּר	speak / discuss	92
דֻּבַּר	to be spoken of	92

ה

Hebrew	English	Page
הָ... / הַ...	the	14
הַבָּא	that is coming	46
הוּא	he	38
הוֹלֵךְ	going (m.s.)	38
הוֹלֶכֶת	going (f.s.)	66
הוֹלְכוֹת	going (f.p.)	66
הוֹלְכִים	going (m.p.)	38
הוֹרִים	parents	46
הִיא	she	38
הָיָה	was	79
הַיּוֹם	today	38
הַכֹּל בְּסֵדֶר	everything is okay	58
הַכֹּל טוֹב	everything is good	58
הֵם	they (m.p.)	40
הֵן	they (f.p.)	40
הִנֵּה	here is	66
הַסּוֹף	the end	66
הִסְטוֹרְיָה	history	86
הַפְסָקָה	break, recess	86
הַרְבֵּה	many	66
הַשֵּׁם שֶׁלִי	my name	38
הַשֵּׁם שֶׁלָךְ	your name (f.s.)	38
הַשְׁמָעָה	sounding / making heard	92
הִתְחַשְּׁבוּת	consideration	92

ו

Hebrew	English	Page
וְ...	and	14
וּ...	and	38
וֵייְז	WAZE	86

ז

Hebrew	English	Page
זֹאת	this/that (f.s.)	14
זֶה	this/that (m.s.)	30
זְמַן	time	86

ח

Hebrew	English	Page
חָבֵר	friend (m.s.)	66
חָבֵרה	friend (f.s.)	38
חָבֵרוֹת	friends (f.p.)	
חָבֵרִים	friends (m.p.)	46
חֶדֶר	room	86
חֲדָרִים	rooms	
חֹדֶשׁ	month	76
חָדָשׁ	new (m.s.)	
חֲדָשָׁה	new (f.s.)	76
חוּץ	outside of (aside from)	76
חוֹשֵׁב	think (m.s.)	92
חוֹשֶׁבֶת	think (f.s.)	76
חַיָּל	soldier (m.s.)	38
חַיֶּלֶת	soldier (f.s.)	38
חִישׁוּב	calculation	92
חָנוּת	store	
חֲנוּיוֹת	stores	66
חָשׁוּב	important / deliberate	92

מילון

כ		
כַּדּוּר	60	ball
כַּדּוּר בָּסִיס (בֵּיְסְבּוֹל)	60	Baseball
כַּדּוּרִים	60	balls
כַּדּוּרֶגֶל	58	soccer
כַּדּוּרְסַל	60	Basketball
כַּדּוּרְעָף	60	Volleyball
כְּדֵי	76	in order to
כִּי	58	because
כֵּיף	66	fun
כָּכָה-כָּכָה	38	so-so
כָּל	76	all
כָּל הַזְּמַן	58	all the time
כַּמָּה	86	how many (much)
כֵּן	22	yes
כֶּסֶף	81	money
כְּתוֹבֶת	86	address
ל		
לְ...	46	to
לְ... /לַ...	38	to the
לֹא	22	no, not
לֶאֱכֹל	52	to eat
לְאָן	58	to where
לְבַקֵּר	52	to visit
לְדַבֵּר	52	to speak
לָדַעַת	52	to know
לָהּ	82	for her, to her
לְהַזְמִין	76	to invite / to reserve
לִהְיוֹת	52	to be
לָהֶם	82	for them, to them (m.p.)
לָהֶן	82	for them, to them (f.p.)
לְהִתְרָאוֹת	46	see you later

חֲשִׁיבָה	92	thought process / thinking
ט		
טוֹב	38	good
טוֹב מְאוֹד	38	very good
טִיּוּל	92	trip / journey
טִיֵּל	92	hike / walk
טַיֶּלֶת	92	promenade / public walk
י		
יָאללָה	46	come on!
יִהְיֶה	76	will be
יוֹם	76	day
יוֹם חֲמִישִׁי	79	Thursday
יוֹם רִאשׁוֹן	79	Sunday
יוֹם רְבִיעִי	76	Wednesday
יוֹם שַׁבָּת	79	Saturday (Sabbath)
יוֹם שִׁישִׁי	76	Friday
יוֹם שְׁלִישִׁי	79	Tuesday
יוֹם שֵׁנִי	79	Monday
יָכוֹל	46	able (m.s.)
יְכוֹלָה	46	able (f.s.)
יְכוֹלוֹת	52	able (f.p.)
יְכוֹלִים	52	able (m.p.)
יֶלֶד	14	boy
יַלְדָּה	14	girl
יָם	38	beach (ocean or sea)
יָמִין	58	right (direction)
יָמִינָה	66	to the right
יָפֶה	30	nice, good, pretty (m.s.)
יָפָה		nice, good, pretty (f.s.)
יֵשׁ	58	there is
יָשָׁר	58	straight
יִשְׂרָאֵל	22	Israel

Dictionary

58	field (sport)	מִגְרָשׁ		82	for him, to him	לוֹ
22	speak (m.s.)	מְדַבֵּר		34	learns (m.s.)	לוֹמֵד
22	speak (f.s.)	מְדַבֶּרֶת		30	learns (f.s.)	לוֹמֶדֶת
	speak (f.p.)	מְדַבְּרוֹת		34	learns (f.p.)	לוֹמְדוֹת
	speak (m.p.)	מְדַבְּרִים		34	learns (m.p.)	לוֹמְדִים
30	what	מָה		52	to tour / travel around	לְטַיֵּל
58	what's happening	מָה נִשְׁמַע		76	to me, for me	לִי
38	how are you(m.s.)	מָה שְׁלוֹמְךָ		76	night	לַיְלָה
38	how are you (f.s.)	מָה שְׁלוֹמֵךְ		38	to the sea	לַיָּם
58	ready (m.p.)	מוּכָן		52	to sleep	לִישׁוֹן
	ready (f.p.)	מוּכָנָה		76	for you, to you (f.s.) 82	לָךְ
66	ready (f.p.)	מוּכָנוֹת			for you, to you (m.s.)	לְךָ
	ready (m.p.)	מוּכָנִים		82	for you, to you (m.p.)	לָכֶם
30	teacher (m.s.)	מוֹרֶה		82	for you, to you (f.p.)	לָכֶן
	teacher (f.s.)	מוֹרָה		52	to go (walk)	לָלֶכֶת
	teacher (f.p.)	מוֹרוֹת		52	to learn	לִלְמוֹד
	teacher (m.p.)	מוֹרִים		82	for us, to us	לָנוּ
76	order(reserve) (f.s.)	מַזְמִינָה		46	to travel	לִנְסוֹעַ
79	tomorrow	מָחָר		52	to work	לַעֲבוֹד
92	taking a walk / excursion	מְטַיֵּל		52	to do / make	לַעֲשׂוֹת
14	who	מִי		52	to buy	לִקְנוֹת
58	water	מַיִם		52	to see	לִרְאוֹת
31	convenience store	מַכֹּלֶת		60	**Ride a bike** לִרְכֹּב עַל אוֹפַנַּיִם	
38	reserves (I.D.F.)	מִלוּאִים		52	to sit	לָשֶׁבֶת
71	restaurant	מִסְעָדָה		58	to play	לְשַׂחֵק
66	restaurants	מִסְעָדוֹת		86	to put	לָשִׂים
79	number	מִסְפָּר		86	to send	לִשְׁלוֹחַ
	numbers	מִסְפָּרִים		92	to hear	לִשְׁמוֹעַ
76	prefer (f.s.)	מַעֲדִיפָה		52	to drink	לִשְׁתּוֹת
76	awesome	מְעוּלֶה			**מ**	
86	interesting	מְעַנְיֵן				
58	from here	מִפֹּה		46	from	מִ... מֵ...
76	place	מָקוֹם		30	very	מְאוֹד
66	center	מֶרְכַּז		46	from where	מֵאֵיפֹה

מילון

58	game	מִשְׂחָק
58	playing (m.s.)	מְשַׂחֵק
	playing (f.s.)	מְשַׂחֶקֶת
66	from there	מִשָּׁם
30	family	מִשְׁפָּחָה
76	when	מָתַי

נ

		נוּ
58	come on (slang)	
92	traveling (by vehicle) (m.s.)	נוֹסֵעַ
	traveling (by vehicle) (f.p.)	נוֹסְעוֹת
92	traveling (by vehicle) (m.p.)	נוֹסְעִים
92	traveling (by vehicle) (f.s.)	נוֹסַעַת
92	a trip or journey	נְסִיעָה
	nice / pleasure	נָעִים
38	very nice (to meet you)	נָעִים מְאוֹד
92	being heard / listened to	נִשְׁמָע

ס

38	awesome	סַבָּבָה
66	end	סוֹף
76	weekend	סוֹף הַשָּׁבוּעַ
31	supermarket	סוּפֶּר
34	student (m.s.)	סְטוּדֶנְט
34	student (f.p.)	סְטוּדֶנְטִיּוֹת
34	student (m.p.)	סְטוּדֶנְטִים
30	student (f.s.)	סְטוּדֶנְטִית
60	fencing (sport)	סַיִף
86	s.m.s. (text)	ס.מ.ס
63	book	סֵפֶר
63	books	סְפָרִים
60	skateboard	סְקֵייטְבּוֹרְד

ע

14	Hebrew	עִבְרִית
66	until	עַד
46	still	עֲדַיִין
30	working/works (m.s.)	עוֹבֵד
	working/works (f.p.)	עוֹבְדוֹת
	working/works (m.p.)	עוֹבְדִים
	working/works (f.s.)	עוֹבֶדֶת
66	more	עוֹד
66	(one more) time	עוֹד פַּעַם
50	standing/stands (m.s.)	עוֹמֵד
50	standing/stands (m.p.)	עוֹמְדִים
50	standing/stands (f.p.)	עוֹמְדוֹת
50	standing/stands (f.s.)	עוֹמֶדֶת
30	doing / do (m.s.)	עוֹשֶׂה
30	doing / do (f.s.)	עוֹשָׂה
	doing / do (f.p.)	עוֹשׂוֹת
38	doing / do (m.p.)	עוֹשִׂים
30	city	עִיר
46	now	עַכְשָׁיו
86	on / about	עַל
46	next to	עַל-יָד
30	with	עִם
76	evening	עֶרֶב
	cities	עָרוֹת

פ

58	here	פֹּה
60	American Football	פוּטְבּוֹל
	turning (f.s.)	פּוֹנָה
	turning (m.s.)	פּוֹנֶה
	turning (f.p.)	פּוֹנוֹת
66	turning (m.p.)	פּוֹנִים
66	time / a time	פַּעַם

צ

38	army	צָבָא

Dictionary

64	theirs (m.p.)	שֶׁלָּהֶם	58	side	צַד
64	theirs (f.p.)	שֶׁלָּהֶן	39	Israeli Defense Forces (I.D.F.)	צה"ל
64	his	שֶׁלּוֹ	76	afternoon	צָהֳרַיִם
14	hello, goodbye, peace	שָׁלוֹם	52	needs (m.s.)	צָרִיךְ
86	three	שָׁלוֹשׁ	52	needs (f.s.)	צְרִיכָה
64	mine / my	שֶׁלִּי	52	needs (f.p.)	צְרִיכוֹת
64	yours (f.s.)	שֶׁלָּךְ	52	needs (m.p.)	צְרִיכִים
64	yours (m.s.)	שֶׁלְּךָ			ק
64	yours (m.p.)	שֶׁלָּכֶם	30	kibbutz	קִבּוּץ
64	yours (f.p.)	שֶׁלָּכֶן	30	kibbutz (plural)	קִבּוּצִים
58	ours	שֶׁלָּנוּ	86	floor (level)	קוֹמָה
38	name	שֵׁם	69	wall	קִיר
58	there	שָׁם	66	walls	קִירוֹת
71	left (direction)	שְׂמֹאל	22	a little (bit)	קְצָת
66	to the left (direction)	שְׂמֹאלָה			ר
92	rumor	שְׁמוּעָה	52	want (m.s.)	רוֹצֶה
86	an hour	שָׁעָה	52	want (f.s.)	רוֹצָה
86	hours	שָׁעוֹת	52	want (f.p.)	רוֹצוֹת
14	language	שָׂפָה	46	want (m.p.)	רוֹצִים
18	languages	שָׂפוֹת	66	street	רְחוֹב
86	six	שֵׁשׁ	60	dancing	רִיקוּד
81	backgammon	שֵׁשׁ בֵּשׁ	60	running (sport)	רִיצָה
86	two	שְׁתַּיִם			ש
		ת	76	that	שֶׁ...
30	thank (you)	תּוֹדָה	46	week	שָׁבוּעַ
83	student (m.s.)	תַּלְמִיד	92	hear (m.s.)	שׁוֹמֵעַ
83	student (f.s.)	תַּלְמִידָה	31	(outdoor) market	שׁוּק
83	students (f.p.)	תַּלְמִדוֹת	60	swimming	שְׂחִיָּה
83	students (m.p.)	תַּלְמִידִים	86	lesson	שִׁעוּר
86	nine	תֵּשַׁע	64	hers	שֶׁלָּה

Advanced Grammar

Hebrew has seven *Binyanim* (Verb forms)

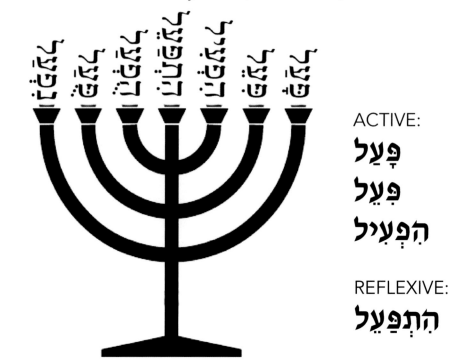

PASSIVE:

נִפְעַל

פֻּעַל

הֻפְעַל

ACTIVE:

פָּעַל

פִּעֵל

הִפְעִיל

REFLEXIVE:

הִתְפַּעֵל

Here is the basic, active verb form - פָּעַל

כ.ת.ב. (write):

Future עָתִיד	Present הוֹוֶה	Past עָבַר	
אֶכְתּוֹב	כּוֹתֵב / כּוֹתֶבֶת	כָּתַבְתִּי	אני
תִּכְתּוֹב	כּוֹתֵב	כָּתַבְתָּ	אתה
תִּכְתְּבִי	כּוֹתֶבֶת	כָּתַבְתְּ	את
יִכְתּוֹב	כּוֹתֵב	כָּתַב	הוא
תִּכְתּוֹב	כּוֹתֶבֶת	כָּתְבָה	היא
נִכְתּוֹב	כּוֹתְבִים / כּוֹתְבוֹת	כָּתַבְנוּ	אנחנו
תִּכְתְּבוּ	כּוֹתְבִים	כְּתַבְתֶּם	אתם
תִּכְתְּבוּ	כּוֹתְבוֹת	כְּתַבְתֶּן	אתן
יִכְתְּבוּ	כּוֹתְבִים	כָּתְבוּ	הם
יִכְתְּבוּ	כּוֹתְבוֹת	כָּתְבוּ	הן

Advanced Grammar

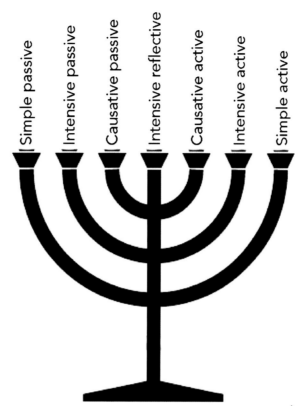

Simple passive | Intensive passive | Causative passive | Intensive reflective | Causative active | Intensive active | Simple active

Here is the basic, active verb form - פָּעַל

Future עָתִיד	Present הוֹוֶה	Past עָבַר	
I will write	writes	I wrote	I
you will write	writes	you wrote	you m.s.
you will write	writes	you wrote	you f.s.
he will write.	writes	he wrote	he
she will write	writes	she wrote	she
we will write	write / write	we wrote	we
you will write	write	you wrote	you m.p.
you will write	write	you wrote	you f.p.
they will write	write	they wrote	you m.p.
they will write	write	they wrote	you f.p.

The End.

This workbook is a Hebrew book and reads from right to left.
The first page of this workbook starts at the other end.

****

Other books by Michelle Geft:

- Read, Write, Recite Hebrew

- Read Hebrew!

- The Aleph Bet Coloring Book

- L'Chaim, The Jewish Holidays in Rhyme
And...

- Roll n' Learn Hebrew, Not Your Classic Dice Game

I always appreciate reviews and it helps learners find and know more about my books.
If you can, please review wherever you bought your book or email me and I can post it
on my web site.

Visit
www.HebrewBasics.com
for free video companions and more.

Thank you very much! !תּוֹדָה רַבָּה